BY THE EDITORS OF CONSUMER GUIDE®

HOME COMPUTERS

Library of Congress Catalog Card Number: 78-63611

This edition published by:
Beekman House
A Division of Crown Publishers, Inc.
One Park Avenue
New York, N.Y. 10016
By arrangement with Publications International, Ltd.
b c d e f g h

Cover Design: Frank E. Peiler
Cover Illustration: C.A. Moberg
Illustrations: Steven Boswick, M.R. LeSueur
Editorial Consultant: Forrest M. Mims, III

Photo Credits: Apple Computer, Inc.; Centronics Data Computer Corp.;
Commodore Business Machines, Inc.; DatagraphiX. Inc.; Digi-Log Systems,
Inc.; Digital Equipment Corp.; Exidy, Inc.; Heath Company; Hew-
lett-Packard; Intel, Inc.; Lear Siegler, Inc.; Monolithic Systems; Pertec
Computer Corp.; Processor Technology; Radio Shack; RCA; Southwest
Technical Products Corp.; Tektronix, Inc.; Teletype Corp.; Texas In-
struments, Inc.; VideoBrain Computer Co.; Xerox Corp.

Contents

What Is a Personal Computer?

EVERYONE READING this has been touched by the computer age, perhaps more than they realize. Your checking account, for example, is probably monitored and updated by a computer at your bank. Your income tax and Social Security records are stored and processed by some of the federal government's largest computers. Some of the dazzling commercials that you see on television are produced by a computer.

If you're a student, chances are your grades, course schedule, tuition account, and library books charged to your name are all stored in your school's computer system. And if you've ever borrowed money or made a purchase on credit, information about you, your financial reliability, and maybe your lifestyle is stored in a computer.

These and many other computer applications touch our lives very directly and often very personally. But the big computers that type much of the junk mail you receive and notify you about your latest credit card billing are not "personal" computers. A personal computer is just that, a computer that is so relatively so inexpensive and so easy to use that a person of average intelligence and moderate means can acquire and use his or her own computer.

Thanks to a remarkable technological achievement in microminiature electronics called the microprocessor, the era of personal computing has finally arrived. The microprocessor is a network of thousands of microscopic electronic circuits etched into the surface of a thin sliver of silicon about the size of the head of a thumbtack.

Silicon, as you may already know, is the main ingredient of ordinary beach sand. It's the material used to make solid-state electronic components such as transistors, integrated circuits (ICs), and solar cells.

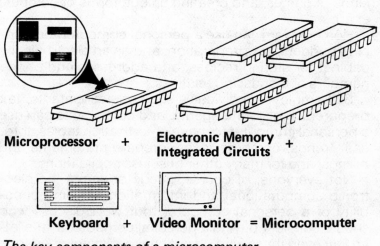

Microprocessor + **Electronic Memory Integrated Circuits** +

Keyboard + **Video Monitor** = **Microcomputer**

The key components of a microcomputer.

One kind of personal computer is made by connecting a microprocessor to a typewriter-like keyboard, an electronic memory, and a television set. The result is a microcomputer or, as personal computer enthusiasts often call it, a micro or, simply, machine.

As for cost, many personal computers are available for about the same price as a good quality stereo system or a large-screen color television set. More sophisticated computers can cost as much as a small automobile, but even some of the more economical personal computers have greater computational ability than those used by scientists during World War II's Manhattan Project to build the first atomic bomb.

Think of the implications! Now the mind-expanding and labor-saving advantages of computers are available to a wide segment of the public. Young people and students can use a personal computer as a sophisticated learning device that can help teach everything from simple arithmetic and creative problem-solving to advanced concepts in computer programming. They can also explore the limitless recreational applications of personal computing by playing and inventing various kinds of games, and creating unique forms of computer art.

Homemakers can use a personal computer for planning budgets, tax preparation, and as an electronic file cabinet for storing recipes, and addresses and phone numbers of friends and relatives.

Self-employed individuals such as accountants, tax preparers, real estate agents, and consultants can use a personal computer to make amortization tables, forecast trends, compute taxes, prepare statements and billings, and for many other business applications.

Not everyone, of course, needs or wants the electronic computational and information-handling capability of a personal computer, but we'll discuss who should consider buying a personal computer a little later. But even those who do not have a distinct need for a

This Apple II is being used to plot stock market averages.

personal computer now would be wise to become familiar with the world of personal computing. Already, microprocessors that are similar or even identical to those used in home computers are found in microwave ovens, calculators, video games, automobile trip computers, washing machines, toys, cameras, and other consumer products. A host of totally new microprocessor-related products and ideas, ranging from robot lawn mowers to electronic mail that is sent and received over telephone lines, is now in the development stage.

Understanding something about personal computing will help you keep up with these sophisticated new products without being intimidated by them. And should you decide to acquire your own personal computing system at some future time, you'll be well prepared to make an intelligent choice.

Computers Are Information Processors

To learn how computers work, it would be best for you to experience a brief session at the keyboard of the typical personal computer. First, however, let's clear up a common misconception about computers.

You already know many things that computers can do, but do you know what a computer is? Most people are misled by the name "computer." They often think that computers are electronic machines that solve arithmetic problems. This is a very incomplete definition. A much better definition is: A computer is an information processor.

A computer can manipulate, sort, erase, and shuffle numbers that are stored in its electronic memory. Since it's a simple matter to let these numbers represent characters and symbols, a computer can electronically organize and remember words. This means that computers can be used for hundreds of applications involving words and, thus, can have nothing to do with arithmetic.

Since a computer is an information processor, it is an amazingly versatile machine. It's like being a combination of a file cabinet, game player, number machine, tax preparer, math teacher, home equipment controller, entertainment device, mind expander, and more.

One reason that computers are well suited for these tasks is their amazing speed. A typical personal computer easily performs a few million operations each second. This fast operating speed, which computer enthusiasts refer to as throughput rate, means that a computer can use relatively inefficient and even clumsy methods to solve complicated problems.

All of these applications and capabilities make computers very impressive technological gadgets. But even the most sophisticated computer is a functionless piece of hardware unless it's been told what to do and how to do it by its human designers and its operator.

Lists of instructions that tell a computer what to do are called programs or software. Well-prepared software can make a relatively low-cost personal computer run circles around a poorly programmed million-dollar industrial computer.

Novice computer enthusiasts are usually surprised to find that it's not essential to know how to program a personal computer to use it. Hundreds of programs are readily available from computer companies, software suppliers, books, and magazines. But thanks to the development of special computer languages, almost anyone can learn simple programming in less than an hour without having access to a computer.

The Altair B-100 CRT terminal displays 24 lines of 80 characters on a nonglare screen.

A Session with a Home Computer

Imagine that you're seated before the typewriter-like keyboard of a personal computer.

Press the key for any letter or number, and the appropriate character instantly flashes on a video monitor. A monitor looks like a standard television set, but it does not generally receive broadcast TV stations. You can type words, sentences, and even fill the entire monitor screen with paragraphs and tables.

So far, our imaginary computer probably seems more like a silent TV typewriter than a personal computer. But the features of this electronic typewriter provide a very convenient and efficient way to give orders to the computer and, in turn, to receive information.

For example, let's say that electricity in your town costs 3.8 cents per kilowatt-hour (kWh), and you want a quick reference table that shows the total bill you must pay for some specified quantity of electrical energy your household consumes. You can work out a table like this with a pocket calculator, but you'll spend a good deal of time pressing buttons and writing down results. A personal computer, meanwhile, will present you with a neatly organized table in less than a second once you've typed a simple list of instructions into its keyboard.

Here's a simple list of instructions that will order a personal computer to prepare your household energy expense table:

```
10 PRINT "KWH", "COST ($)"
20 FOR X = 0 TO 500 STEP 50
30 PRINT X, X * .038
40 NEXT X
```

After you've typed these instructions into your imaginary computer, type RUN and the table will be flashed on the computer's screen:

KWH	COST ($)
0	0
50	1.9
100	3.8
150	5.7
200	7.6
250	9.5
300	11.4
350	13.3
400	15.2
450	17.1
500	19

Our energy cost program is very basic. In fact, it's written in a language that many computers understand called BASIC. And though you don't have to understand BASIC (Beginner's All-Purpose Symbolic Instruction Code) to use a personal computer, virtually all computer users soon pick up the fundamentals of BASIC and even learn to write their own programs.

Let's look at the energy cost program again. Notice that each of the lines or steps in the computer's instruction program begins with a number. We could have used 1, 2, 3, 4, but 10, 20, 30, 40 means that we can insert new steps directly into the program without having to erase and retype the original steps.

Now let's discover what each step in this sample program does:

10 PRINT "KWH", "COST ($)": This "typewritten" line provides some labels for the energy cost table. PRINT is a BASIC instruction that tells a computer to flash any following words or symbols inside quotation marks on the computer's video monitor. The comma between "KWH" and "COST ($)" tells the machine to separate these items by several character spaces when they are displayed.

Now look at the second step:

20 FOR X = 0 TO 500 STEP 50: This tells the computer that we want to look at the cost for 0 to 500 kilowatt-hours in steps of 50 kilowatt-hours. Labeling the number of kilowatt-hours with an "X" is a shortcut that allows the computer to keep track of what the current number of kilowatt-hours is.

Here's the third step:

30 PRINT X,X* .038: You already know that PRINT tells a computer to display anything on the same line that's within quotation marks. PRINT can also be used indirectly to tell the computer to display any requested information. In this case, the information is "X" (the number of kilowatt-hours) and "X" multiplied by .038 (the cost per kilowatt-hour). Incidentally, the computer indicates multiplication with an asterisk because "X" is often used to indicate a number.

The final step is simply:

40 NEXT X: When the computer runs the program , it automatically calculates the cost for O kWh and prints the result on the screen. NEXT X tells the computer to advance to the next value for "X," in this case "50" (the instruction STEP 50 in line 20) and repeat steps 20 and 30.

If you're new to computers and programming, you might not completely understand how our simple energy cost program works. But with a little practice, most people soon surprise themselves with their computer programming abilities. That's because the modern personal computer is an amazingly forgiving machine. If you include an incorrect procedure in your program (a bug in computer jargon), the computer will notify you about the error by flashing "WHAT?" or some other error signal after you type RUN. It will even show you exactly where the error is located! Naturally, this speeds up the process of perfecting a program, a procedure computer programmers call debugging.

Even if you haven't the slightest idea how our simple

energy cost program works—and don't care to learn at this stage—you can still make full use of it. You can probably find a much more elaborate version of the energy cost program at a library or computer store, too. For example, we can easily amend our simple four-step program to do all this:

1. Calculate and display the cost for any number of kilowatt-hours consumed.

2. Add any energy adjustment charge.

3. Figure the sales tax and add it to the subtotal for each number of kilowatt-hours used.

And, we could even have the program keep track of your energy expenses on a monthly basis, keeping you informed about your energy consumption habits with a bar graph electronically painted on the computer's display monitor.

See how versatile a computer, even a personal one, can be? And, we've barely begun to use the incredible capabilities of our imaginary machine!

A good pocket calculator, however, will easily handle almost anyone's calculating needs. Quality programmable calculators, like those made by firms such as Texas Instruments and Hewlett-Packard, can even solve a wider range of mathematical problems than some personal computers that cost hundreds of dollars more. Personal computers, however, are much faster and easier to program. For example, in a comparison test between a Hewlett-Packard Corporation's HP-25 pocket programmable calculator and Radio Shack's Level-1 TRS-80 personal computer, the computer, in terms of sheer calculating ability, was no match for the HP-25's powerful mathematical and scientific capabilities. But for repetitive programs, involving the four basic functions of addition, subtraction, multiplication, and division, the computer solved problems much faster than the calculator.

To determine exactly how much faster, the HP-25 and TRS-80 were programmed to add all the numbers

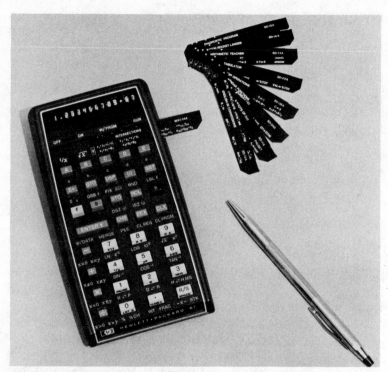

This Hewlett-Packard 67 calculator stores and reads programs from magnetic cards.

between 1 and 1000 (1 + 2 + 3 + 4 + 5 . . . + 1000 = ?) . The calculator program for this operation was nine steps long and required a total of 15 keystrokes. The TRS-80 program required only four lines of BASIC and about twice as many keystrokes. The HP-25 took 4 minutes, 10 seconds to solve the problem. The TRS-80 flashed out the answer on its screen after only 10 seconds! In case you're wondering, both machines gave the correct answer—5050.

But suppose that you're not interested in arithmetic, much less having an expensive computer do something as trivial as figure your electric bill or balance your checkbook. This is where a computer parts company with even the fanciest pocket calculators. As we observed earlier, a computer can remember words, phrases, names, addresses, telephone numbers, and even recipes. And, it can sort or rearrange information like this in virtually any way you specify. In short, a personal computer can function as an electronic memo pad that will store, arrange, tabulate, and manipulate information that you type into it.

How It All Began

Computers are the end result of a complaint most of us have had at one time or another about the time required to solve arithmetic problems. Arithmetic was invented when prehistoric mathematicians figured out clever ways to count with their fingers, toes, pebbles or knots tied in a string. So people have had plenty of time

An experienced abacus operator can add and subtract at least as fast as a person using a calculator.

to devise shortcuts in arithmetic.

Ingenious ways to perform arithmetic with fingers and pebbles were invented thousands of years ago. The most famous of these is the abacus. Even in this age of readily available, low-cost calculators, the abacus remains an important calculating machine in countries like Japan and China. American businessmen are often startled to see their highly educated Asian counterparts pull a well-used abacus out of the desk when it's time to strike a deal.

An abacus may appear clumsy to the uninitiated, but a skilled operator can solve many arithmetic problems on an abacus faster than with an electronic calculator. How can finger-propelled beads move down a rod faster than electrons can zip through the electronic brain of a calculator? They can't. But an experienced abacus user can flick beads as fast as pressing the keys of a calculator. And, since he doesn't have to press an "equal" key to arrive at an answer, the abacus often wins in a race against a pocket calculator.

So the abacus is a fast way of solving arithmetic problems once you've learned to use it effectively. But it requires years of practice. In 1642, Blaise Pascal, a teen-aged French mathematician, anticipated this problem. Bored with hours of repetitious calculations, Pascal invented a machine that could add and subtract with the help of wheels marked with the digits 0 through 9 around their rims. Each wheel had a tab that moved the wheel to its left a tenth of a revolution for each complete revolution of the wheel on the right. Pascal's ingenious invention is still in use as the odometer in most autos and the counter on some tape recorders.

Mechanical addition and subtraction were just not enough for another bored mathematician. In 1671, Gottfried Wilhelm Leibniz built a machine that multiplied and divided. And, in the early 19th Century, Charles Babbage designed the "Analytical Engine," a sophisticated machine that in many respects resembled a modern digital computer.

The first electronic computers were developed in Germany, Britain, and the United States during World War II. One of their primary uses was to calculate artillery tables.

By 1946, ENIAC (Electronic Numerical Integrator and Computer), the first really sophisticated computer had arrived. It was the biggest electronic device of its time. ENIAC was so big that a room the size of a small house was needed just to contain its 30 tons of switch-studded control panels, half a million solder connections, and nearly 20,000 vacuum tubes. Those tubes required an immense amount of power, 200,000 watts to be exact, but they could add two numbers together 5000 times in a single second.

Shortly after the ENIAC was in use, some Bell Laboratories scientists invented the transistor, a pea-sized

Early computers filled rooms with expensive equipment.

electronic component that could do most things that vacuum tubes do with a lot less power. At first, transistors were very expensive and not too reliable. By the late 1950s, however, the hot, fragile and short-lived tubes used in computers were being replaced with more reliable, cool-operating, inexpensive and long-lived transistors. The new transistorized computers were smaller, about the size of a desk, and cheaper (hundreds of thousands instead of millions of dollars).

Transistors are made by imprinting electrodes on tiny chips of silicon. In the early 1960s, several scientists devised a way to form half a dozen transistors on the same silicon chip. The result was the integrated circuit (IC) that made it possible to squeeze networks of dozens of transistors into a plastic package not much bigger than a single transistor.

In 1965, integrated circuits were used to make the first minicomputer, an $18,000 machine no bigger than a two-drawer file cabinet. For the first time, many colleges, small businesses, and research laboratories could afford their own computer system.

Since then, many kinds of minicomputers have been developed, but the most important advance in computer technology today is the microprocessor. This is a silicon integrated circuit chip with several thousand microscopic circuits that form the electronic nerve center of every personal computer.

The first microprocessors cost several hundred dollars each. This sounds expensive, but, remember, a single microprocessor and a handful of other components substitute for thousands of electronic parts. Like most other new electronic technologies, however, microprocessor prices have plummeted. Today, a microprocessor complete with a microscopic memory—sometimes called a complete computer on a chip—can be purchased for less than $10.

Applications for the new generation of microprocessors and microcomputers are popping up everywhere.

But their most important application is as the electronic brains behind personal computers. Today, the computing power of the mammoth ENIAC is available to anyone with less than $600 to spend. And, much less than that if you do not want that much power.

The personal computer represents a striking contrast to ENIAC. A typical low-cost personal computer has more parts on the surface of a tiny silicon flake no bigger than a watermelon seed than ENIAC had tubes. Yet today's computer has a thousand times fewer solder connections, and probably consumes less power than the lamp you're using to illuminate this page.

While today's personal computer is only five or 10 times faster than ENIAC, it's fast enough. And, it is much easier to use and considerably more reliable. ENIAC had a habit of blowing several tubes each time it was turned on. And, a personal computer is no bigger than a combination typewriter-TV set. Some are considerably smaller.

Microprocessor chips are available for less than $10.

How Computers Compute

THE BEST way to understand how a computer computes is to learn something about how its component sections are organized. This isn't nearly as difficult as it might seem, because every computer can be divided into five major sections: control, arithmetic, memory, input, and output.

Chances are that you probably own an electronic calculator. Since calculators are miniature computers for the task of solving arithmetic problems, even the cheapest one has each of these sections. Often the arithmetic, control, and memory sections are com-

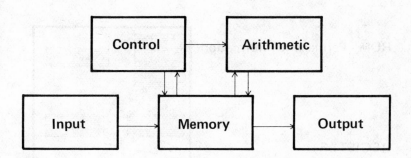

These are the five major sections of every computer.

bined on a single integrated circuit chip. The arithmetic and control sections form a microprocessor, and the memory provides the information storage that transforms the microprocessor into a very limited computer.

Let's discuss each of these sections and learn what they are and how they work.

INPUT—The keys that permit you to enter numbers and various instructions (like add, subtract, multiply, and divide) form a calculator's input. When the calculator is turned on, its circuits continually scan each of the keys one at a time to see if any have been pressed. When a pressed key is found, the calculator goes into action.

MEMORY—Calculators have at least two kinds of memories, both of which are made from arrays of transistors on the integrated circuit that forms the machine's electronic brain. One memory is called a read-only memory, or ROM for short. It contains a permanent set of instructions that tells the calculator how to solve problems.

The second kind of memory is called a register. Two registers are assigned to remember numbers that are keyed into the keyboard. A third register stores the re-

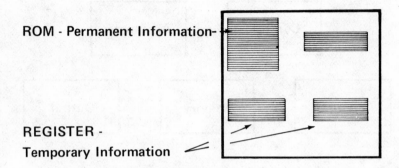

ROM - Permanent Information-

REGISTER -
Temporary Information

A calculator's memory circuits are placed on its microprocessor chip.

sult of a problem. Since information can be written into and then read out of a register, it's sometimes called a read-write memory or random-access memory (RAM).

Unlike ROMs, the information in a register can be changed. If power is turned off, the register loses any information that is stored in it.

ARITHMETIC—The calculator's arithmetic section is a complicated maze of transistors that can add two numbers. It's possible to subtract, multiply, and divide by adding. The calculator's ROM stores the instructions that tell the calculator how to do all these things and whatever else the calculator is designed to do (like squaring a number, extracting the square root of a number, etc.) by repeated addition.

CONTROL—The electronic nerve center of every calculator and computer is the control section. Control is busier than a traffic cop during rush hour as it reads the information that's been punched into the keyboard, fetches instructions on what to do with the information from the ROM, interprets or decodes the instructions, and orders the arithmetic section to per-

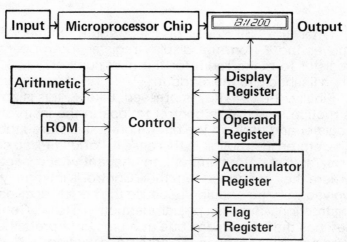

This depicts how the sections in a calculator are organized.

form whatever is necessary to process the information and instructions that are keyed into the keyboard.

OUTPUT—The row of digits that displays the numbers entered into a calculator and the results of calculations form the calculator's output. Some calculators also have a small paper printer that provides a permanent record of calculations.

Both calculators and computers follow a similar procedure to solve simple arithmetic problems. So let's follow a simple "four-banger" (add-subtract-multiply-divide) calculator through its paces. Here's how the machine adds 2 + 3 = 5:

Control constantly scans the keyboard to see if any keys have been pressed. When the "2" key is pressed, control responds by loading a 2 into the display register. This register is connected directly to the calculator's display so a "2" is flashed into the readout.

The "+" key is pressed next. Since this is an instruction key that tells the calculator what it is supposed to do, control stores a binary code for + in a special instruction register.

When the "3" key is pressed, control immediately moves the 2 from the display register to an operand register to make room for the new number. A "3" is then flashed into the readout.

Finally, the "=" key is pressed. Like +, this is an instruction key. It tells control to look in the instruction register and perform the operation that is stored there. The stored instruction in this case is "add" (+), so control moves both numbers to the arithmetic section where they are added together. Control is intimately involved with the addition because the adder receives its instructions from a special instruction ROM. Control fetches the instructions one at a time, interprets them, and passes them on to the arithmetic section.

The sum is then moved to the display register and a "5" glows in the display. The sum is also stored in a special register called the accumulator where it's available to be combined with other numbers.

Now that you've seen how a calculator goes through the steps necessary to perform a simple addition problem, you're well on the way to understanding how a computer operates. Calculators, however, are much more limited than computers. Most of them can only perform a limited number of functions. Most computers can do everything a calculator does plus lots more.

Inside a Computer

Most personal computers are amazingly versatile machines. Many different kinds of input and output devices can be connected to them. They can be given extra memory. They can be programmed to solve a virtually unlimited variety of problems. And, they can process characters, symbols, and words in addition to numbers.

Earlier, we discussed the five sections in the pocket calculator, a very simple computer. Now let's examine each of these sections as they're found in a general-

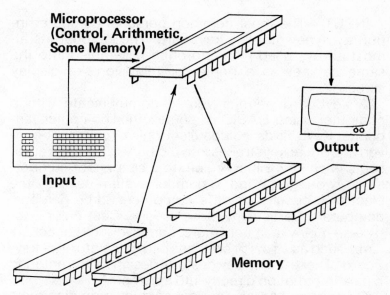

This depicts how the main sections of a computer are organized.

purpose personal computer.

The operation of a computer is centered around a microprocessor, but its various sections are considerably more versatile than those in a calculator. Also, a computer usually has more memory circuits than those available on the limited space of the microprocessor chip.

All this is why personal computers are often called systems. Like a quality stereo system, many different extras or options can be connected into the system to provide enhanced operating performance.

Later we'll cover some of the personal computer options that are available in depth. For now, however, let's briefly introduce each of the sections in a personal computer to learn something about what they do and how they work.

INPUT—The most common personal computer input is a typewriter-like keyboard. The keyboard is almost always used with and often assembled into the same cabinet as a printer or television-like display screen.

A keyboard permits you to communicate with a computer using BASIC or some other computer language. Keyboards include electronic circuits that convert individual keystrokes into a binary code that represents each key. Binary refers to a simple but cumbersome two-digit (0 and 1) number system used by the electronic circuits inside a computer. Some personal computers, particularly those used by electronics hobbyists, employ a much more primitive input mechanism, such as a row of switches or a calculator-like keyboard. These input devices are designed for entering binary information directly into a computer.

Computers can also be connected to an electronic circuit that converts variable or analog information such as temperature, wind speed, and gasoline flow into binary form. These circuits are called analog-to-digital (A/D) converters. They allow a computer to respond to many different situations without the need for a human operator. They're connected to the computer through a special connection called a port.

MEMORY—The most important and expensive part of a computer is memory. Programs and other information that are typed into a computer's keyboard are stored in a temporary memory called a read-write memory or RAM. A RAM is like an array of hundreds or even thousands of registers in a calculator. Each register in the RAM stores a binary number as long as power is applied or until a new number is written over the former one.

Like calculators, computers also have ROMS or read-only memories. One ROM is located right on the microprocessor chip that forms the electronic brain of a personal computer. This ROM is very similar to a cal-

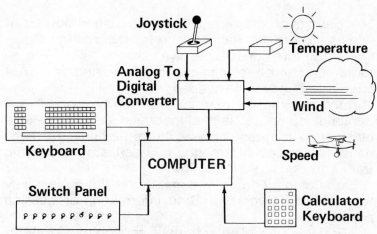

These are several types of computer inputs.

culator ROM since it tells the microprocessor how to do what it's instructed to do by the keyboard.

Another ROM may be located on one or more integrated circuit chips that are separate from the microprocessor. It contains a special program that converts the English words and phrases used in BASIC into the binary instructions called machine language that the microprocessor understands. The program is called an interpreter or compiler, depending on the conversion method it uses.

Some hobbyist-style home computers that use switches instead of a typewriter-like keyboard for an input section have a special ROM that automatically sets up the computer for various operations when the power switch is turned on. This can save the several minutes of switch flipping that are required to manually enter the necessary information. A ROM program like this is called a bootstrap loader.

All personal computers include both RAM and ROM memory. Many also include a way to connect an ordinary cassette tape recorder directly to the computer.

This permits programs and even information like lists of names, addresses, recipes, and tax records to be permanently stored on inexpensive cassette tapes. The information can be read back into the computer's RAM memory whenever it's needed.

Another external memory that can be added to a personal computer is the magnetic disk. A flexible plastic disk that resembles a 45 rpm record, the magnetic disk stores information in a series of concentric tracks around its surface.

Expanding a computer's memory is the easiest way to increase its versatility and information-processing power.

ARITHMETIC—The arithmetic section of a computer is much more flexible than that of a calculator. It can process more bits of information at any one time so it requires fewer steps to perform arithmetic operations. It also has the ability to do various logical, or decision-making, operations. For example, it's often necessary for a computer to take one of several courses of action, depending on the status of a particular number or pair of numbers. The arithmetic section includes circuits that can compare numbers and inform the computer if they are equal and, if not, which is the greater number. These same circuits can make many other decisions.

CONTROL—The control section of a personal computer is even busier than the control section of a pocket calculator. Control fetches instructions from the memory, interprets them, and shows the other parts of the computer how to do whatever is necessary to fulfill the instructions.

Control spends lots of time interacting with the arithmetic section. That's why both of these sections are assembled together on a microprocessor chip. Together, they're called a computer's central processing unit or CPU. Since the development of the microprocessor, it is also called a microprocessing unit (MPU).

Control also spends a great deal of time fetching

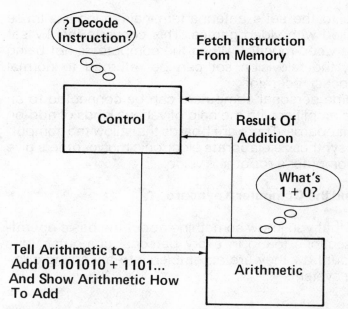

Control and arithmetic form a computer's central processing unit (CPU).

instructions from the computer's control ROM. Placing the control ROM on the microprocessor chip greatly simplifies computer design and speeds up processing operations, too.

OUTPUT—A computer's output section provides a way for transferring information processed by the computer to the outside world. As mentioned earlier, many personal computers use a printer or a TV-like screen for an output. The television display is called a video monitor. Sometimes, both an input keyboard and a video monitor are assembled into a cabinet along with the rest of the computer to provide a compact, often portable, personal computer system. Some personal computers are designed to be connected directly to a television set by means of a special module that connects to the set's antenna terminals much like those supplied with video games. This converts the TV set into a video monitor. When the computer is not being used, the television set can be returned to normal broadcast reception.

Some personal computers can be connected to an audio amplifier with the help of various kinds of add-on circuit boards. There are boards that allow the computer to synthesize elaborate electronic music; others give the computer a robot-like voice.

Behind the Computer Keyboard

Now that you know something about the basic operating sections found in every personal computer, let's find out how they are assembled into a working computer system.

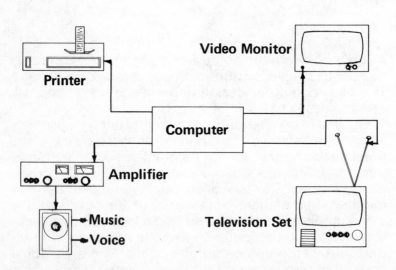

Some output devices that are used with computers.

PRINT "HELLO"

FOR X = 0 TO 100

NEXT X

. . .01101011

. . .11001101

. . .01101001. . .

Computers can process only the 0s and 1s of the binary number system.

Binary Numbers and Logic Gates

Personal computers are amazingly complex devices, but the most complicated, the biggest, and the costliest computer made today has much in common with an ordinary light switch. Its circuits consist of an elaborate maze of electronic switches called logic gates. Like a light switch, the logic gates in a computer can be only on or off.

At first it's difficult to believe that on-off switches can be used to make a computer. A switch can be in only one of two positions: on or off. That means we can represent only the first two of the 10 digits of the decimal number system we're accustomed to using.

But why limit ourselves to using decimal numbers? Why not use a number system that can be expressed with on-off switches?

That's exactly what the engineers who design computers have done. They selected a very simple number system with only two digits. It's called the binary number system, and its digits, or bits as they're called, are "0" and "1." Though it's possible to communicate with a personal computer using everyday words, symbols, and numbers, all the information fed into a computer or stored in its memory must be converted into the binary language of "0's" and "1's."

Most people, professional computer programmers included, find the binary number system very awkward at first. That's to be expected, since the decimal system is much more sophisticated and everyone has been trained in its use. On the other hand, the binary number system is much simpler than the decimal system. Believe it or not, you must memorize 100 rules to add any two decimal numbers together! Binary addition only requires four rules.

What are those 100 rules for decimal addition? They're so ingrained in your mind that you probably don't think of them as "rules." But the rules for decimal addition are all the possible ways to add any two of the digits 0 through 9. Make a table, count the combinations, and you'll arrive at 100. Sure, some combinations are repetitious (2 + 3 and 3 + 2) and others do not seem very important (0 + 0 and 5 + 0), but each combination is a rule.

Here are the four rules for adding binary numbers:

$$0 + 0 = 0$$
$$0 + 1 = 1$$
$$1 + 0 = 1$$
$$1 + 1 = 0, \text{ carry 1 or 10}$$

You can memorize the rules for binary addition in less than a minute, yet these rules allow you to add any two binary numbers. And that's not all. Subtraction is the reverse of addition. Multiplication is nothing more than repeated addition, and division is repeated subtraction.

This means that any arithmetic or mathematical problem can be solved by various combinations of addition, subtraction, multiplication, and division. Therefore, any mathematical operation can be solved with the help of the four rules for binary addition.

Now let's return to the switch. Earlier, we noted how a switch is either on or off. If we let the binary bit "0" correspond to "off" and the bit "1" to "on," we can express binary numbers electrically.

It's very easy to use transistors as on-off switches. Transistor switches are turned on and off by very small electrical signals instead of a mechanical handle or push button. This means that transistors can be switched on and off by other transistors and, in turn, switch still other transistors on and off.

Several transistor switches can be connected together to form circuits called gates that can make simple yes-no decisions. One such circuit is called the AND gate. The switches that detect when one or more seat belts in a car are not fastened form a simple AND gate. Each belt acts like an on-off switch.

If one or both belts is unfastened, a buzzer buzzes. If the driver's belt *and* the passenger's belt are fastened, the buzzer is silent.

As you can see, this combination of two switches can make a simple yes-no decision.

Another common decision circuit is the OR gate. Of-

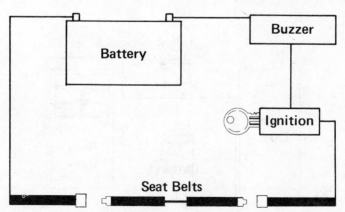

A car's seat belt warning system is a simple AND gate.

ten a light or doorbell can be turned on by either or both of two switches. In this case the switches form an **OR gate. The light** (or doorbell) is turned on if one switch *or* the other switch is turned on.

One other type of gate is very important to computers. It's called the inverter or NOT gate. It has one input point and one output point. A "0" fed into the NOT gate is changed to a "1"; a "1" is changed to a "0."

This simple gate is not very important on its own. But combine it with an AND gate and you get a NOT-AND or NAND gate. Combinations of NAND gates can be used to make any other computer gate. Incredible as it may seem, a complete digital computer can be made from only NAND gates.

Automobile companies use only a couple of basic chassis designs for every car they build. Personal computers, however, are much like high fidelity systems. They are built using a wide variety of methods. As you will see, the method used to assemble a computer can directly affect how many options or peripherals can be added to a particular machine.

The one construction method, however, that is common to all personal computers is the printed circuit

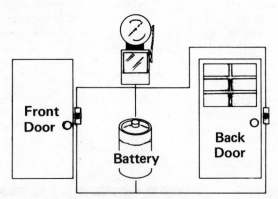

A door bell operated by two switches is a simple OR gate.

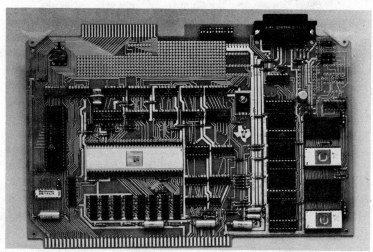

This is a computer circuit board with a microprocessor, memory integrated circuits and other components.

board. The microprocessor and various integrated circuits that allow the microprocessor to communicate with a keyboard, video monitor, and the computer's memory are installed on a circuit board or card. The board contains metal patterns that take the place of wire to connect the various components to one another. The components are mounted on the board by soldering their pins into holes on the foil pattern. The result is sometimes called a module.

The precision nature of a computer's printed circuit board can contribute substantially to the cost of a computer. Most boards have printed wiring patterns on both sides. These double-sided printed circuit boards are difficult to make and, consequently, are fairly expensive.

Some very limited personal computers have only a single circuit board. More advanced computers include a second board or card containing additional memory integrated circuits, usually RAMs.

What You Can Do with Your Own Computer

BY NOW, one of the most important questions that you're probably asking yourself is, "Do I need my own computer?" In a way, it's like asking if you are willing to trade in your wonderful little pocket calculator for a scratch pad and pencil. Like automobiles and airplanes, and radio and television, we have done without such inventions for centuries. But the "luxuries" of past decades have a habit of becoming the necessities of the present, and we wouldn't think of doing without them now. Even the computer is rapidly becoming an indispensable part of running a smaller business.

One difference between the personal computer and all those other inventions is that the personal computer is not yet regarded as a necessity. But those who know about computers now will be way ahead of the pack because one day they'll be commonplace in the home. Whether it's a necessity for you probably depends on the answer to a second question: "What are some of the specific things I can do with a computer?"

Someone has estimated that there are at least 25,000 computer applications waiting to be discovered, and as one publication noted recently, asking what are the applications for the computer "is like asking what are the applications for electricity."

Computers are amazingly versatile machines, and we know a lot of the things that personal computers are able to do. But whether you can get one to do these things is another matter, and we ought to discuss this important detail before we explore some of the practical and specific things that personal computers can accomplish.

If you're shopping around in one of the computer retail stores spread around the country, some overenthusiastic salesperson may be tempted to dazzle you with the possibilities of this remarkable device. But when you finally take a computer home with you, it doesn't necessarily perform certain functions without your assistance. Whether we're talking about business computers or personal computers, you cannot ignore one inescapable fact about them: They all have to be programmed, which simply means that somebody has to tell them how to go about doing their jobs.

Obviously, that someone is the person who uses it. If he doesn't know how, he has to learn or find someone who does. There are generally two types of personal computer users. One knows how to program a computer to do whatever he wants it to do, or he can eventually figure it out. He may already be a professional programmer, a hobbyist who likes to experiment, or an individual who just likes to find out how computers go about doing their jobs.

The other type of user has neither the skill to program a computer nor the inclination to learn it. Somebody else can handle the details. He just wants results.

One user can probably create most of his own programs—software, as it is called. Another user has to depend on someone else for software—maybe someone like the first user, or anyone else able to program a computer, even though that someone else may not own a computer. There are many people who can create software with varying skill but, of course, they want to be paid for what they create. In any case, if you can't do or plan to learn to do your own programming and you're thinking about buying a personal computer, don't leave this consideration out of your calculations.

There are other sources of computer programs. These include computer manufacturers, software suppliers, and magazines, among others. But compared to the potential applications of the personal computer, available software at a modest cost has a long way to go.

Manufacturers have started a small library of prepackaged software in the areas of computer games, personal finances, education, and art, but there is not too much else. Yet, as the personal computer market grows, it is inevitable that many companies will be producing computer programs to turn appliances on and off, activate lawn sprinklers, monitor the doors and windows of a home while a family is away, adjust the heating system for the most efficient use of energy, and so on.

These are control functions that require, besides the software, additional "hardware" to link the computer to the system it is controlling. If you're into electronics, you'll probably be able to rig up some kind of gadget for this purpose, but most people will have to spend anywhere from $50 to $150 for extra hardware, depending on the application. Some of this hardware is commercially available; some is not. But like the software, as the market grows, the hardware will multiply.

Before going on to some computer applications, let's pause and sum up.

The personal computer is potentially able to do many things, but don't be misled by advertisements that promote exciting but impractical applications for your situation. Instead, try to identify the applications that interest you and the hardware and software that they will require.

Now let's examine some of the things personal computers can do. Keep in mind, however, that a reasonably priced computer with a keyboard and a video monitor will handle many of the applications described. And, that it is possible to reduce the cost of a personal computer by using a home television set as the monitor. Some applications, meanwhile, may require additional equipment, such as an expensive disk memory system or a costly printer to produce a written record of the computer's work.

Fun and Games

A few years ago, a company making pocket calculators that can be programmed like a small computer asked its customers what they liked most about the product. Being mostly engineers, physicists, and educators, they naturally replied that they were quite impressed by the mathematical power of the device. But a good number of these very learned customers admitted that they often used their calculators as a portable entertainment center, amusing themselves with computer games.

Long ago, computer users discovered that creating and playing computer games is not only a lot of fun, but an excellent way to improve one's programming skills. It's no surprise, then, that personal computers spend part of their working lives entertaining people with games and other diversions. Much of the software currently available is of this type. The personal computer has so many recreational uses, including those that you can create yourself, that we cannot possibly cover them all. But we can look at some of the more popular ones.

Let's begin with old standbys such as tic-tac-toe, checkers, nim, and chess. And you're probably familiar with numerous video games that involve boundaries, goals, nets, players, paddles, bouncing balls, and so on. Most personal computers can create games like these. While some computers cannot produce the visual detail of a TV game, others can generate pictures with at least the same quality, and some with considerably more detail.

More than picture quality, however, distinguishes video games from computer games. Those played on a computer provide greater variety and can be more involving. Most TV games offer you a selection of games, but you have to play by one set of rules for each game. And, the rules cannot be changed. Playing games with a computer, on the other hand, is much more fun because the players can change the rules to suit their whims, making the games easier or more difficult. On top of that, the player and the computer can communicate with each other while they play!

It is true that some video games are becoming more sophisticated, with built-in microcomputers that make them, in effect, a mini-version of a personal computer. But as entertainment devices, even these cannot compete with the personal computer, which, when properly programmed, computes odds, keeps score, predicts the eventual winner, and taunts you with witty comments on your lack of game-playing prowess.

The Electronic Palette

Many computer owners can express themselves artistically through their personal computers. You say that you can't even draw, much less paint? Don't worry. You don't need to. You can be the owner of an instant art school; and a computer unit, keyboard, and video monitor can become your palette, brush, and canvas.

For example, take Apple Computer, Incorporated's Apple II personal computer, a unit that is able to generate 16 colors including black and white. Connect it to a color video monitor or your home color TV and you'll soon be creating your own masterpieces. Not traditional art, to be sure, but intricate patterns of color and shape that can intertwine and change as they appear and move across the screen. The complexity of computer art is limited only by the sophistication of your programming. If you wish to preserve your artistic creations, you can do so by storing your programs on a cassette tape recorder.

Your Personal Tutor

Flash cards are often used to drill young students in basic arithmetic. But like other tasks learned by rote, flash cards can be boring. How interesting would a teacher be who did nothing but hold up signs for a pupil

A personal computer can make learning fun by commenting on a pupil's progress, or lack of progress.

to read with no response, no feedback, and no involvement?

A personal computer can make the task of learning arithmetic fun by serving as an electronic deck of flash cards, but with a twist. And the twist makes the difference between passively staring at signs and getting involved in the process of learning. Programs of this kind are now available. The computer flashes a problem for the pupil on its display screen. The pupil types his answer on the keyboard. His or her answer appears on the screen, and the computer comments on the answer.

Here's how a typical computerized learning sequence might look:

Computer: Hi! What's your name?
Pupil: Randy.
Computer: Nice to meet you, Randy. Today we're going to practice the multiplication tables. You'll have a minute to answer each problem. Are you ready to begin?
Pupil: Yes.
Computer: What's 4 x 7?
Pupil: 32.
Computer: Sorry, Randy, that's not the correct answer. Please try again.
Pupil: 28.
Computer: Very good! Now, what's 6 x 9?

The computer goes on presenting problems for a period of time fixed by the program or until the pupil turns off the unit. Some computers are able to produce an infinite series of mathematical problems, so that the program could go on indefinitely. But whenever the learning session ends, the computer flashes the number of correct answers on its screen, pays the pupil a compliment for a good score if it is deserved, or, if not, suggests that more study is needed.

Computers can teach more than arithmetic. Since

their unfailing memories can hold a mine of data—names, dates, places, events, words, phrases, and numbers, to list only a few types—computers provide an excellent means of teaching factual information in history, languages, economics, government, and many other subjects.

Educational software for personal computers is available, making it likely that in a few years do-it-yourself tutoring with a personal computer will be a major mode of learning certain kinds of material.

Household Problem-Solving

In economic terms, a family can be regarded as a small business. It brings in money and pays it out. It has a budget, invests in equipment that it must replace over the years, keeps a running inventory on the raw material it uses, makes interest-bearing loans, pays taxes to the government, and so on. And, like any good business, a family should have an efficient way to manage this activity.

The personal computer can perform household chores, such as keeping track of the family budget.

Take the simple task of balancing a checkbook. Even a low-cost personal computer can do the job. For that matter, a pocket calculator can do it. But once your personal computer begins to manage your checkbook balance, you might as well have it keep track of the family budget. Whenever you ask, the computer will flash on its screen a neatly itemized comparison of budgeted expenditures with actual expenditures, and show the differences between them. Computerizing a family budget might at first seem like overkill, but while stimulating you to save, it keeps track of those expenses that are tax-deductible.

And speaking of savings, you can use a personal computer to quickly assess the earnings that you will receive by investing your money in various savings plans. Sure, a pocket calculator can also do this, but you'll have to maintain a lot of notes. The computer does away with all that, displaying on its screen a well-organized comparison of investment plans. And, it can analyze them in ways that would take you hours or even days on a calculator.

Keeping inventories, like balancing checkbooks, comes naturally to the personal computer. Would you believe the computer can automatically subtract the groceries you use each time you prepare a meal from your kitchen inventory? At your command, the computer can also produce a printed grocery list—if your system has a printer—that will allow you to replenish your grocery stocks in a single trip to the store and eliminate costly impulse buying.

Suitable software can provide the kitchen with even more sophisticated help, like planning menus, automatically adjusting recipes for the number of people you plan to serve, planning diets, and so on.

In the last few years, most people have come to realize that the days of cheap and abundant energy are over, at least for the foreseeable future. How can the personal computer reduce your household energy budget and save precious energy? Simple. It allows you to carefully study all the methods of saving energy that are available to you. For example, take insulation. If you already have six inches of fiberglass insulation in your attic, is it cost effective to add more? Should you add storm windows and more insulation throughout your home with money you might invest at a greater profit somewhere else? Ask your computer. It is capable of giving you sound, objective advice to help you decide.

Eventually, personal computers will be preparing individual income tax returns, much as computer service companies are doing for accountants' clients today.

Lemonade Computer Companies

How would you like a free personal computer? It can be done. With the right kind of computer system and a little imagination, you can start your own one-person business—a kind of electronic "lemonade stand," as *Popular Computing* magazine likes to describe this concept. Your computer can pay for itself and make money in the bargain. And, if your fledgling business meets IRS requirements, it could even qualify for some tax deductions, including depreciation allowances, operating expenses, and so on.

Here are a few ideas for your "lemonade stand." Maybe they will stimulate you into thinking up others.

You might rent your computer. After spending all that money, why risk renting it out? Why not? All you need to do is set aside enough space in your home for the computer and rent it to users by the hour. Leave the programming up to your customers. You can generate business by posting announcements of your service in computer stores, computer clubs, and schools. Some of your customers may include people who want to see how your computer works before they buy their own.

How many times have you gotten a "personal" letter from a land developer, a credit card company, a charity, a promoter, or a politician? That letter was probably typed by a computer. Some home computer owners have more than paid for their equipment by preparing "personalized" advertising letters for local offices and businesses. The client's form letter is typed into the computer's memory with the spaces for names and addresses left blank. A separate list of names and addresses is also typed into the computer. From then on it takes over, automatically composing copies of the letter addressed individually to the people contained in the list.

A variation of the personalized ad campaign is the family newsletter. Many people like to exchange newsletters with their friends at holiday time. Why not offer a personalized newsletter service? Your customers supply the text of the newsletter along with the names and addresses of those who are to receive it. You and your home computer do the rest.

Since computers are ideal for organizing, storing, and retrieving information, one way to get your computer to pay for itself is to use it as an automated clearing-house for miscellaneous information. Let's illustrate this with a simple example, say, a garage sale. People all over town conduct garage sales, but a buyer looking for a particular item has to wander all over looking for it. You and your computer can simplify this problem immeasurably and make money at it. The seller arranges with you for your service, publicizes it in his ads, and mails you a list of the items for sale. You store the information in the computer. Now, suppose a buyer wants a bookcase. He calls you and you enter "bookcase" into the computer. Within seconds the screen flashes the addresses of all garage sales with bookcases for sale. The seller then pays you a commission on all sales derived from your service.

Such a data clearinghouse can be set up for countless transactions of this kind, from real estate to used cars; in fact, for the rapid retrieval of any information that people are willing to pay for.

The opportunities for creating software are limitless for the computer programmer who knows what he is doing. Some users of personal computers have become very adept at writing programs for interesting games or unusual applications. The widest market for software in the future, of course, will be the one that fills the practical needs of the public. Computer companies are always looking for useful software they can sell, and computer magazines for programs they can buy and publish. So if you enjoy programming and are good at it, this is an excellent way to earn money. And, while doing so, you can develop your skills for a possible career.

Many of the reasonably practical things that are being done with personal computers today have been covered and some of the limitations have been discussed. As you've seen, they lie not so much in the computer's capacities as in the person who will operate it and the shortage of software. Earlier, it was emphasized that the personal computer will perform any chore asked of it as long as the request is made in a language that it understands. But you have to know more than just how to press all the buttons and flip all the switches. You've got to know the language or have a program already in that language. Obviously, this is important if you're thinking about getting yourself a personal computer. But it won't be long before the market will be flooded with programs and the hardware that they require to do things we probably haven't even thought of yet.

As in any new technology, the changes will be rapid, both in the equipment and the prices. At one time the simplest electronic calculator sold for several hundred dollars. Now, a basic calculator can be bought for less than $10. The personal computer will follow this pattern. It will surely drop in price, though not as dramatically as the pocket calculator.

Getting Started in Personal Computing

IF YOU think that it's necessary to own a computer to enter the world of personal computing, think again. Thanks to the proliferation of computer clubs, educational courses, magazines, books, and manufacturers' literature, a person can become very involved in personal computing without owning his own machine.

This chapter covers some of the ways that you can get started in personal computing, whether you elect to buy your machine now or later. Let's begin by analyzing your present and future needs.

Do You Really Need a Computer?

You might expect that a book about personal computing would encourage every reader to rush out and buy a computer. But some readers may neither need nor can afford the luxury of possessing their own computer. With this in mind, every potential home computerist should face the question: "Do I really need and can I afford a personal computer?"

Think about this for a moment. What applications do you have in mind for your own computer? Do you want the business-oriented capabilities that some personal computers offer or are you more interested in fun and games? Or do you want a trainer-type computer so that you can learn computer fundamentals first hand, at low cost, before buying a more sophisticated machine?

Personal computers are not necessities of life. But, of course, neither are most other modern electronic equipment such as calculators, digital watches, and color organs. All of these technological goodies can enhance our lifestyle, but the personal computer is in a special category. It can open up an entirely new world of intellectual, educational, and recreational opportunities. It can add entirely new and mind-expanding dimensions to the way that you conduct business, play games, learn, organize your finances, and communicate.

Defining the Personal Computer

An essential step for becoming involved in personal computing is defining the personal computer. In the broadest sense, personal computers can include such microprocessor-based products as calculators, advanced video games, handheld games, microwave oven controllers, fuel adjustment systems for automobiles, dashboard-mounted trip computers, and other devices.

Some of these products, particularly the advanced programmable calculators that are now available, certainly qualify as limited personal computers. Here, however, only those computers that are general purpose in nature are being considered.

In contrast, advanced programmable calculators are primarily used for solving mathematical problems, though many calculator users enjoy inventing games to play with their machines. Some of these calculators can solve a much more impressive array of mathematical problems than can a lower-level personal computer. Indeed, unless you need the much faster and more advanced programming options offered by a computer, you probably will be better off selecting a much more affordable and portable pocket calculator if your only application is solving mathematical problems.

For processing and storing words, increased programming capability, and the wide range of applications described in the previous chapter, you will have to move up to a general-purpose personal computer. Several major categories of personal computers are available, so let's define each of them.

What Kinds of Personal Computers Are Available?

The novice computerist is faced with a bewildering variety of personal computers. Fortunately, virtually all personal computers can be lumped into three categories:

1. Consumer computers
2. Appliance computers
3. Hobby computers

Briefly, both consumer and appliance computers are supplied ready to use. All that's required is to plug a power cord into a wall outlet, connect a couple of clips to the antenna of a television set (unless the computer is supplied with a video monitor), and turn on the power. Appliance computers, though, are much more sophisticated than the more limited consumer variety.

Hobby computers, often available as kits, are designed for the do-it-yourselfer who enjoys electronic construction and wants to put together his or her own system. Most hobby computers are at least as sophisticated as a typical moderately priced ($500-750) appliance machine. Moreover, they can also be used for business or industrial purposes.

The costs, capabilities, construction methods, and versatility of the various computers within each category vary widely. There is also considerable overlap between the categories. Therefore, it's important to understand the major capabilities, differences, and drawbacks of the computers within each category before selecting a personal computer.

What follows is a breakdown of the various categories along with some important guidelines to help you classify personal computing systems.

Consumer Computers

Consumer computers are the simplest and least sophisticated of personal computers. Designed for mass consumer appeal, they are an extension of the video game. Consequently, do-it-yourself programming is deemphasized in favor of libraries of prerecorded program tapes.

A typical consumer computer costs between $200 and $500, comes equipped with either a calculator- or typewriter-like keyboard, and is housed in a plastic cabinet. In operation, the unit is connected to the antenna terminals of a black and white or color television set like a video game. A program cartridge is then selected and inserted into the machine. The TV screen then flashes out the instructions necessary to implement the selected program, such as "SELECT THE GAME YOU WISH TO PLAY BY TYPING ITS NUMBER INTO THE KEYBOARD: 1. SPEED QUIZ; 2. TIC-TAC-TOE; 3. NUMBER GUESSER."

Since the programmability of the consumer comput-

The VideoBrain is one of the first consumer computers.

ers that are now available is very limited, the usefulness of these machines is almost totally dependent on the manufacturer's software library. VideoBrain, one of the first consumer computers, is supported by a library of cassette tapes containing programs that teach music, spelling, simple arithmetic, and very simple programming concepts using a combination of tests, questions, and color graphic effects. Other programs in the library permit checkbook balancing, price comparisons, and metric conversion. There are also several multicolor games.

Consumer computers are the newest entry in the personal computer market, and only a few models are now available. Some of these machines may prove popular with consumers who can afford the relatively expensive software, typically $20 for a single-program cartridge.

The prospective buyer of a personal computing system, however, should take a close look at appliance and hobby computers before making a purchasing decision. While consumer computers offer color graphics, joysticks, and other video game spinoffs, their computational ability is not nearly as powerful as that of some similarly priced appliance computers. And, they can be used only for applications defined by the expensive software cassettes available, at least for now, only from the manufacturer.

Appliance Computers

The appliance computer is a fully programmable, general-purpose machine that understands BASIC or some other higher-level computer language. Like consumer computers, prerecorded program tapes can be used with appliance computers. Their programmability, however, makes appliance machines considerably more versatile.

Appliance computers range in cost from about $600 for Radio Shack's TRS-80 to several thousand dollars or more for a sophisticated system suitable for use in a business.

Numerous peripherals or extras are available for appliance-level computers. They include disk memories, RAM memory modules, various kinds of printers, and expansion modules that permit a computer to be connected to these and other extras.

Few appliance computers use the standardized "bus" connections that characterize many hobby computer products. Several companies, however, sell adapter circuits that permit an appliance computer to be connected to a wide range of otherwise incompatible products.

Until recently, the only way to acquire a personal computer was to enter the complex world of hobby computers. The arrival of low-cost, sophisticated appliance computers will attract many more new computer

The Apple II is one of the first appliance computers.

enthusiasts who haven't the time, desire or ability to build their own computer system. For example, how many people do you know who have built their own color television set from a kit?

Nevertheless, it's essential that serious enthusiasts keep their eyes on the booming hobby market. Virtually every appliance computer and peripheral had its origins in or was stimulated by the hobby market. In other words, today's hobby computer or peripheral is tomorrow's appliance computer or peripheral. Also, many peripherals originally designed for use with hobby computers can be used or adapted for use with an appliance computer.

For these reasons, be sure to familiarize yourself with hobby computers even if you're primarily interested in appliance computing.

Hobby Computers

Credit for the arrival of the era of personal computing rightfully belongs to the electronics hobbyist. Shortly after the first microprocessors became commercially available, experimenters and hobbyists began devising ways to use them in homemade computers.

In July 1974, *Radio-Electronics* magazine published the assembly plans for the Mark 8, a primitive do-it-yourself microcomputer. Then, in January 1975, *Popular Electronics* ushered in the era of low-cost personal computing with an article that described how to build the powerful, modestly priced ALTAIR 8800 microcomputer, designed by MITS, Inc.

These do-it-yourself computers were very inexpensive, but an upward trend has occurred as manufacturers continue to introduce increasingly sophisticated circuits to perform wide-ranging applications. Today, the price of a kit computer can easily exceed that of a ready-to-use appliance machine! The kit machine may not have significantly more computational abilities than the preassembled unit, but it is often considerably easier to expand.

A chief reason for increases in price and sophistication of kit computers is that many so-called hobby computer companies have found that a substantial number of their customers are not hobbyists at all. One firm surveyed its customers and found only 10 percent were bonafide hobbyists. The bulk of its sales were to small businesses and educational and research institutions that were eager to take advantage of the substantial cost savings offered by hobby computers having as many features and capabilities as much more expensive minicomputers. Furthermore, many electronic enthusiasts use hobby computers wholly or partially for personal use while depreciating them for business tax purposes.

Like consumer and appliance computers, a hobby computer's microprocessor and the various integrated circuits that allow the microprocessor to communicate with a keyboard, video monitor, and the computer's memory are installed on a card called a double-sided circuit board. Thin metal patterns on both sides of the card connect the various integrated circuits.

The SWTP CT-64 computer terminal is an advanced hobby computer kit.

Often, the connection points for the keyboard, video monitor, memory, and the power required by the board are organized into a row on both sides along one edge of the card. The row of connections, which is called a bus, is inserted into a special socket in the computer's cabinet.

Some computers may have a row of a dozen or more card sockets in the bottom of a box-like cabinet. Each connection point on a socket is wired to the same point on all the other sockets. Since a socket usually has 50 or 100 connection points, wiring a dozen sockets together can require up to 1200 individual solder connections.

The requirement for soldering all these connections by hand can be eliminated by inserting all the sockets in a special circuit board called a mother board. The mother board has a thin metal pattern that connects all the socket positions. All the sockets are simultaneously soldered to the mother board by passing the board

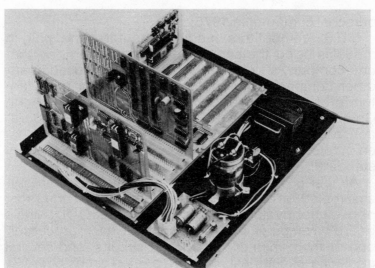

This is an internal view of a hobby computer showing plug-in circuit boards and a mother board.

over a wave of molten solder in an automated soldering machine.

Some hobby computer companies offer preassembled and soldered mother boards that greatly simplify the assembly of a hobby computer system. Though the various circuit boards that are plugged into a mother board to make a computer are available factory-assembled, some hobbyists prefer to build the boards themselves.

Hobby computers are supported by a wide range of both kit and assembled plug-in circuit modules that provide such unique capabilities as enabling a computer to speak with a robot-like voice, synthesizing electronic music, creating patterns on the display of a video monitor, and understanding human speech.

Many of the electronic connections to these add-on circuit models are organized according to the S-100 bus. This connection method was popularized by MITS, Inc., the company that introduced the first viable personal computer in 1975.

MITS' competitors made computers and plug-in modules using the same connection pattern, so that one company's products could be readily used in another company's computer. Several major manufacturers of kit personal computers, notably the Heath Company and Southwest Technical Products Corporation, do not use the S-100 bus, but for more than a dozen others, the S-100 has become the de facto industry standard.

Almost all hobby computers are available factory-assembled or as do-it-yourself kits. One of the most popular hobby computers is the preassembled "single board" computer that consists of a microprocessor, one or more memory integrated circuits, and several additional circuits installed on a printed circuit board.

Many different single-board computers are available. Often, a small calculator-style keyboard and digital readout is installed on the board as well. The keyboard and readout allow the hobbyist to enter pro-

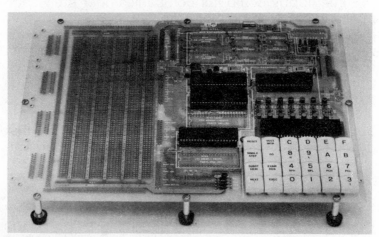

The SDK-85, based on Intel's 8085 microprocessor, is a typical single-board hobby computer.

grams in the machine language that the computer understands. Connections on the board allow most single-board computers to be connected to such peripherals as a video monitor and printer.

Single-board computers represent the best bargain in hobby computers. Many industrious and inventive hobbyists have put together sophisticated personal computing systems based on a low-cost, single-board computer. Do not purchase a single-board computer, however, unless you have some knowledge or are interested in learning about electronics. Although various extras are available for some of these computers, you're on your own when it's time to connect them to the computer.

How Much Computer Should A Beginner Buy?

Suppose you have analyzed the advantages to be had in owning your own personal computer, evaluated your financial situation, and decided to consider purchasing a machine. Let's further assume that you are reasonably familiar with the three categories of personal computers and have decided to select an appliance or hobby micro. The question at this point then becomes "how much computer should I buy?"

An appliance-level personal computer complete with keyboard, processor, some memory, and a video display can be bought for about $500 to $600. A machine in this class can handle a reasonable amount of the BASIC computer language and will keep the home computerist busy for quite some time. But, as we'll soon see, more powerful computers and dozens of accessories are available that can rapidly run the expense of a personal computing system to thousands of dollars. Some of the "personal computer" companies, for example, have even begun to offer "small business systems" for more than $10,000!

So the question "how much computer should I buy?" is of prime importance to the prospective personal computer owner. Fortunately, most personal computers are like many cameras and high-fidelity systems. You can start with a relatively limited micro and expand it with peripherals such as a printer, disk memory or additional RAM as new requirements arise and your finances permit.

Although peripherals can be added to most personal computers, it's important to know that, with the exception of hobby computers, there is very little compatibility between products made by various personal computer companies.

Some manufacturers of small business computers use a standardized "bus structure" that permits add-on modules made by computing companies to communicate with one another. As mentioned, a bus is the row of electrical connectors along one side of a printed circuit board that is inserted into a socket in a computer. Most consumer and appliance computers do not use a standardized bus structure. The range of peripherals that can be added to a particular computer might therefore be limited to those made by the company that makes the computer and possibly a few "parasite" companies. Parasite companies, which have evolved into a kind of personal computer cottage industry, make add-on circuit boards and other products designed to be used with computers made by other, usually larger, companies.

Some companies make interface circuit modules that permit otherwise noncompatible computers and peripherals to communicate with one another. Such a module can permit a low-cost appliance computer, supported by a relatively narrow range of peripherals, to be used with many of the peripherals originally designed for hobby computers.

With all these points in mind, we can now answer the original question by saying that you should buy only as much computing power as you need and can afford when you make your purchase.

You might strike a better deal on a package deal that

includes a variety of options and peripherals in addition to the computer. But remember that as competition increases and new products arrive on the market, you may be able to purchase the peripherals you need when you need them for an even greater savings.

For this buying strategy to work, however, you must select a computer supported by a relatively wide range of peripherals or extras. Ideally, the peripherals should be available from more than one firm.

Naturally, this strategy places a very low priority on consumer-level computers and emphasizes appliance and hobby machines. Computers in the latter two categories are far more versatile and easier to expand than relatively primitive consumer computers. Furthermore, few, if any, parasite companies make peripherals for consumer computers. This restricts the future expansion of a consumer micro to only those products made by the company that made the computer.

Learn More About Computers

By reading this book, you have already demonstrated your interest in learning about personal computers. If you are serious about personal computing and want to derive as much benefit as possible from your own personal computer, you should begin now to learn as much as you can about the subject before you buy one. You will soon surprise yourself at how much you can discover about what may now appear to be an impossibly difficult subject.

The best way to learn about personal computers is to read everything you can find on the subject. Read this book first—all of it! Then, buy some computer magazines and read them. Buy some books about personal computing, or obtain some from a public library. Read computer club bulletins and newsletters. Send for brochures and literature from personal computer companies to learn about what is available. Read the advertisements in computer magazines.

Fortunately, plenty of descriptive literature about personal computing is readily available. Let's review some personal computing magazines and books.

Personal Computer Magazines

We've already noted how *Radio-Electronics* and *Popular Electronics,* two magazines aimed at electronics hobbyists, experimenters, and technicians, formally ushered in the era of personal computing with articles describing how to assemble the Mark 8 and the ALTAIR 8800 hobby computers. Both of these publications have continued to publish articles describing new do-it-yourself computers, and if you are one of those who enjoys building your own equipment, be sure to check out these monthly magazines. *Popular Electronics* is known for its regular introduction of new technology computer products.

For cover-to-cover coverage of personal computing topics, you can select from a half dozen or more new magazines that have appeared in the last few years. Some of these magazines are very technical in nature and are primarily intended for the advanced computer hobbyist. Others are for the "end user," the person who has little or no interest in what goes on behind the keyboard of a personal computer.

Personal computer magazines are available by subscription or at computer retail stores. Some libraries subscribe to one or more of them. Be sure to browse through several recent back issues of a magazine before subscribing to it to make certain that your needs and interests coincide with its contents.

Here is a brief description of some important magazines devoted wholly to computers:

BYTE (Published monthly by BYTE Publications, Inc.; 70 Main Street, Peterborough, NH 03458; single issue: $2; annual subscription: $15.)

The first magazine dedicated entirely to the computer hobbyist, the first issue of *BYTE* appeared only six months after *Popular Electronics* published the now-famous ALTAIR 8800 construction article. In case you're wondering, *BYTE* takes its name from the term used to describe a computer "word" having eight bits. Most hobby computers are built around microprocessors that process information in 8-bit chunks or "bytes."

A typical issue of *BYTE* is 200 pages in length and contains detailed technical articles on many different hardware and software aspects of appliance- and hobby-level personal computers. Book reviews, owners' reports about various computers, new product listings, and club information are also included.

Computer (Published monthly by the IEEE Computer Society; 345 East 47th Street, New York, NY 10017; single issue to nonmembers: $6; contact society for membership information.)

Serious personal computerists should have a look at this quality publication. While primarily aimed at institutional and business computers, the magazine recently has included plenty of information about personal computing. The March 1977 issue, for example, was dedicated to small-scale computing.

Creative Computing (Published bimonthly by Creative Computing; P.O. Box 789, Morristown, NJ 07960; single issue: $2; annual subscription: $15.)

Creative Computing is written for the software enthusiast rather than for the hardware-oriented hobbyist. Its claim that it publishes more software applications than any other personal computing magazine is certainly accurate. Applications that are covered include computer art, music, artificial intelligence, speech synthesis, games, sports simulation, puzzles, investment analysis, and others. It also includes product reviews, fantasy, fiction, and social commentary. Even casual computer enthusiasts should have a look at a copy. Many of the ideas, articles, and programs that it contains are truly mind-expanding.

Dr. Dobb's Journal Of Computer Calisthenics And Orthodontia (Published 10 times a year by Dr. Dobb's Journal; El Camino Real, Box E, Menlo Park, CA 94025; single issue: $1.50; annual subscription: $12.)

Dr. Dobb's Journal is one of the few computer magazines that is supported solely by subscribers. Having no advertisers, it is free to throw darts at inferior products and manufacturers who fail to keep their promises about delivery dates and service. In its own words, the journal "regularly publishes joyful praise and raging complaints about vendors' products and services." In addition to product reviews, *Dr. Dobb's Journal* provides in-depth coverage of the software scene. It's definitely not a hardware-oriented magazine like *BYTE* and others.

Interface Age (Published monthly by McPheters, Wolfe & Jones; 16704 Marquardt Avenue, Cerritos, CA 90701; single issue: $2; annual subscription: $14.)

Similar to *BYTE,* but simpler and easier to understand, with good graphics. A good magazine for both beginning and more experienced computer hobbyists.

Kilobaud (Published monthly by Kilobaud Co.; 73 Pine Street, Peterborough, NH 03458; single issue: $2; annual subscription: $15.)

A spin-off from *BYTE, Kilobaud* is very similar in quality and content. The magazine is better organized, however, and articles are easier to find. Like *BYTE,* Kilobaud is a must for serious computer hobbyists.

Mini-Micro Systems (Published monthly by Cahner's Publishing Company; 270 St. Paul Street, Denver, CO 80206; single issue: $2; annual subscription: $25; free subscriptions available to corporate managers and engineers who meet certain qualifications.)

This magazine is primarily intended for the professional who wants to stay abreast of the latest developments in small computer systems. Many products described, however, are compatible with both appliance and hobby personal computers. A column by prominent microcomputer expert and author Adam Osborne, "Busman's Holiday," reports on developments in personal computing.

People's Computers (Published bimonthly by People's Computer Company; 1263 El Camino Real, Box E, Menlo Park, CA 94025; annual subscription: $8.)

This tabloid-style periodical is dedicated primarily to end-users. It carries BASIC programs for various applications including games. Its hardware articles are proposals and suggestions for new equipment rather than "how-to" construction projects. It always manages to provide its fair share of highly opinionated letters and editorial comments.

Personal Computing (Published monthly by Benwill Publishing Corporation; 1050 Commonwealth Avenue, Boston, MA 02215; single issue: $2; annual subscription: $14.)

This well-illustrated, slick monthly receives high marks for its general contents. Aimed at the end-user rather than the dedicated electronics hobbyist, a typical issue includes perhaps a dozen BASIC programs, an article or two on how to make money with your micro, news about developments and products in the field of personal computing, several tutorial articles, and perhaps a piece or two of fiction.

SCCS Interface (Published monthly by Southern California Computer Society; P.O. Box 54751, Los Angeles, CA 90054; annual subscription: $15, includes membership.)

This is the official publication of the Southern California Computer Society, but it's widely read throughout the United States. The periodical carries a good mix of technical and nontechnical articles. In the latter category are product evaluation reports of interest to anyone preparing to purchase an appliance- or hobby-level computer. It also contains news and information about SCCS events and personal computing activities in southern California.

Personal Computer Books

A flood of new books about both the hardware and software aspects of personal computing has recently arrived on the scene. A few of these books, particularly those about software, are for the general reader. Most, however, are aimed at the serious do-it-yourselfer.

Some of the software books are quite good and belong in every personal computerist's library. A few of these books are described in the "Where To Find Programs" chapter.

Many of the new hardware books have been rushed into print to meet the burgeoning demand of armies of computer enthusiasts. Consequently, their editorial quality varies widely.

It's not possible to review all the new books about personal computing here. However, the following is a selected list of books that have been favorably received by most reviewers:

An Introduction To Microcomputers, Volume 0—The Beginner's Book by Adam Osborne. (Adam Osborne & Associates, Incorporated, 1978, $7.50.)

An excellent book for the beginner who wants to learn about computer operation and terminology. Plenty of illustrations and simple explanations of complicated concepts.

An Introduction To Microcomputers, Volume I—Basic Concepts by Adam Osborne. (Adam Osborne & Associates, Incorporated, 1977, $7.50.)

If you want to know how a microprocessor works, this best-selling book is for you. It's heavy reading for beginners, but most reviewers agree that it is the best tutorial description of how microprocessors work and how they are programmed.

An Introduction To Microcomputers, Volume II—Some Real Products by Adam Osborne. (Adam Osborne & Associates, Incorporated, 1977, $7.50.)

This book is an indispensable reference to the do-it-yourselfer who wants to design and build his own computer system. It describes all the most common microprocessors now available.

Getting Acquainted With Microcomputers by Louis E. Frenzel, Jr. (Howard W. Sams and Company, 1978, $8.95.)

This 288-page handbook is aimed at those who are primarily interested in hobby computing. It covers the operation of microprocessors in detail and includes sample programs. It also describes many of the single-board training microcomputers that are on the market.

The author is director of computer and educational products for the Heath Company and while he does cover Heath's personal computer products, the book presents a rather objective treatment of the field. It is must reading for serious hobby computer enthusiasts as well as beginners who want to learn as much as possible from a single volume.

Microcomputer Primer by Mitchell Waite and Michael Pardee. (Howard W. Sams and Company, 1977, $7.95.)

An ideal book for the novice computer hobbyist with some previous electronics experience (perhaps construction of a Heathkit). The book covers basic computer concepts, hardware, and programming in the machine language understood by microcomputers. The hardware and programming chapters may seem overly technical to the beginner. They are, however, much simpler and easier to understand than similar sections in most other books about microcomputers.

Understanding Digital Computers by Forrest M. Mims, III. (Radio Shack, 1978, $3.95.)

This large-format book is designed as a self-learning text for the beginner. Though the book is organized into 10 conventional chapters, the reader is encouraged to skip around and read those chapters that interest him most before tackling more difficult ones. The text is supplemented by numerous photographs and figures. Dozens of question-and-answer checkpoints scattered throughout the text permit quickie reviews and self-testing.

Understanding Digital Electronics (Texas Instruments Learning Center, $3.95).

Many books about personal computing assume some knowledge about electronics on the part of the reader. This book is an ideal primer for those who want to learn something about digital electronics before tackling a personal computer book. If you are primarily interested in software and if you plan to purchase ready-to-operate equipment for your own personal computing system, you can get by without a knowledge of digital electronics. But hobby computer enthusiasts and those who would like to know more about how the circuits in a computer operate should definitely acquire a copy of this 265-page book.

If your knowledge of electronics is weak, have no fear. This book uses very simple explanations and clear diagrams to explain even very complicated ideas.

Your Own Computer by Mitchell Waite and Michael Pardee. (Howard W. Sams and Company, 1977, $1.95.)

This 80-page paperback is an ultra-simple primer that virtually anyone should be able to read and understand with little or no difficulty. It's ideal for the beginner with no previous computer experience.

It is, of course, only a primer. Readers who become interested enough to consider purchasing their own computer should consider reading a few more advanced books before making a decision.

Remember, these books are only a representative cross section of the dozens that are available. Most computer stores carry a wide selection of books about personal computing. A few personal computer books are also available at libraries.

Where To Buy Your Computer

THE QUESTION of where is the best place to buy a personal computer is of crucial importance, particularly since the personal computer field is still in its infancy. Fortunately, there are several options, ranging from retail department stores to the new marketing phenomenon of retail computer stores. You can also buy personal computer systems by mail order. Or, you might want to consider obtaining a used computer for a bargain price. Each of these purchasing options has advantages and shortcomings. Let's examine each of the alternatives in more detail.

Retail Department Stores

Already, some low-power personal computers, the so-called appliance or consumer variety, have made their appearance next to video games, pocket calculators, digital watches, and other electronic exotica now available at a very few retail department stores. This marketing trend is expected to grow.

Due to their purchasing power, retail department stores will be able to offer some excellent personal computer buys. This sounds good so far, but there can be major pitfalls in buying your machine from a department store. Let's look at some of them.

Have you ever purchased a pocket calculator capable of more than simple addition, subtraction, multiplication, and division from a department store clerk? If so, you've probably run into the future shock ailment called "I—really—don't—know—that—much—about—how—it—worksitis."

Not being able to keep up with idiosyncrasies of the latest product of the digital electronics revolution is not necessarily the salesperson's fault, either. New calculators with more and fancier features are announced so often that it's all but impossible for a salesclerk to learn how all of them operate. But if you've had trouble finding out how a new calculator works from a department store clerk, wait until you try to buy a computer.

Don't misunderstand. This is not a put-down on salespeople. Some salespeople that you'll meet will no doubt be very informed about the operation of the computers they sell, particularly if they sell only one or two models. But many will simply not have the time or desire to become knowledgeable about the products. So, unless you know of a department store with qualified computer salespeople or unless you've already decided on a particular computer after looking over product literature, don't rely on retail department stores for knowledgeable advice about personal computers. Moreover, product choice is very limited.

When you buy an automobile, all you get in the way of software support is an owner's manual. You get that with a computer, too, but a computer has infinitely more operating possibilities than a car.

Unless you're a skilled and experienced computer programmer, you should expect to receive at least some software support (printed programs, programs on cassette tape, etc.) where you buy your computer. Some computer companies that sell their machines through big retailers will provide software—for a price, of course. Department store computers usually are appliance-grade. Therefore, the software might be too limited for the applications you have in mind, particularly if you plan to eventually expand your machine by adding extras.

Retail department stores are not in a position to carry all the computer extras or peripherals that are available. The capital expenditure is just too high. What is worse, many appliance computers, the kind usually sold by department stores, can be connected only to peripherals made by one or perhaps a few companies. This means that your options for expansion are limited to what few peripherals are available.

If your television set goes on the blink, you can quickly find a list of TV repair shops in the yellow pages. Within a few minutes, you can assemble several repair estimates and select a particular shop. But what happens if the screen of your brand new "Super Brain 1000" flashes into oblivion during a fast and furious game of "Space Wars"?

If your machine is under warranty (and that's what we'll discuss next), you can send it back to the manufacturer for repair. But what if the warranty has expired? Then what do you do?

If you bought the machine at a retail department store, you can probably forget about taking it back in for repair. And your local TV repair shop wouldn't be able to fix it either. Repairing a computer can sometimes be a very complex undertaking. So what do you do? Unless the machine's manufacturer offers out-of-warranty service, you will have to take your "Super Brain 1000" to a good computer store and hope they have the ability—and desire—to look it over for you. Chances are, though, that they'll not be nearly as interested in servicing your department store special as the brand of equipment purchased by their customers. In short, personal computers are by far the most complex consumer products on the market. Repairing them can be a very tedious and specialized job. And, retail department stores are simply not set up for this service at this time.

Whether or not a computer is adequately warranted should be of paramount concern to you, the potential customer. Personal computer warranties are discussed in more detail later. For now, however, it's important to understand that a defective machine under warranty must often be returned to the manufacturer, not the store where you bought it, and at your expense. Don't depend on a sales pitch either. Make sure you read the actual warranty, and that you get a copy of it with the machine.

Mail Order

Would you believe you can order an entire computer system by mail or even by telephone, and have the works delivered to your door by a big brown United Parcel Service truck?

If you're confident of your computer selection and if the price and warranty are right, mail order can be an excellent way for you to acquire your own system. The choice of products is widest here. There are, however, at least three drawbacks to buying computers this way.

First, make sure you place your order with a well established, reputable firm. Some personal computer companies have been known to announce a spectacular new product before it was fully evaluated and ready for production. The result was hundreds of customers sending in thousands of dollars worth of orders for a product that's not ready to be shipped. Usually, after a delay of months and a string of mailed explanations ("We're sorry for the delay, but an unexpected design problem has..."), the merchandise is received.

If a computer product you want isn't available locally, mail order is a good source of equipment, but make certain that you know something about the company you're dealing with before you place your order. Read computer magazines, ask around at computer club meetings, find someone who's ordered something from the same company. And never plunk down your money until you know you'll get prompt delivery!

Secondly, you are responsible for checking out the computer system and making sure it works. That's no problem if the machine works properly. And it usually will. But if the machine is defective and if you're new to computing, it might take you some time to discover the problems.

Third, unless the mail order computer company has a nearby repair center, you'll have to ship your machine back to the factory if it needs repair. This, of course, is also one of the disadvantages of buying from retail department stores, and it leads us to the third and, for most people, best choice for buying a personal computer.

Computer Stores

Unless you plan to purchase a relatively low-powered appliance machine, the best place to buy a personal computer is from a local computer store.

In October 1975, Lois and Richard Heiser opened the world's first personal computer store in Santa Monica, California. They named their pioneering enterprise The Computer Store. At that time, most people had never heard of a "personal computer." They gave the store almost no chance for success. But never underestimate the commercial potential of the inexpensive computer. The Heisers' store has been a phenomenal success. The number of employees has more than doubled and the enterprise has expanded into much larger facilities.

The Computer Store was first in what has now become one of the most significant retailing phenomena in recent years. Now there are literally hundreds of computer stores scattered across the United States. Every major city, and plenty of smaller ones, have at least one. Some have a score or more.

Think of the benefits that computer stores offer. You can see and operate the latest personal computers before making a purchasing decision. Unlike department stores, you're usually not limited to one or two models either. And you can ask questions to your heart's content because computer store salespeople (who are often part owners of the store) are by their very nature and background quite knowledgeable about the products that they sell. You might have to wait in line, though. Some stores are literally jammed with customers eager for a few minutes at the console of a demonstration model.

In short, computer stores are generally the best place to buy all but the lowest-grade appliance computers. Here are some of the reasons for this conclusion:

Most computer stores carry several different lines of personal computers. This means you can conveniently compare the features, capabilities, and physical appearance of competing machines, all with the help of a knowledgeable salesperson.

If you think you're getting a snow job, you can return to the store at a time when more customers are there. Computer lovers are compulsive talkers, and they usually delight in any opportunity to expound on the merits, and especially demerits, of competing machines. Don't pin your decision completely on the advice of a "computer store groupie," though. But do consider it as one more data input before making up your mind.

Most computer stores carry a full line of add-ons like printers, extra memory cards, floppy disks, and special-purpose circuits for the machines that they sell. This is important if you think that you'll some day want to expand the capabilities of your own computer. It means that you can get a "hands-on" evaluation of various peripherals and options even before you buy your machine.

Unless you're an experienced programmer, or plan to become one on your own, it's important to determine how much software is available for the computer you plan to buy before you spend your money.

Computer stores are almost always staffed by people who know a lot about hardware and software, and they can offer plenty of advice on what's available. Lots of software is free for the asking (try your local library for books about BASIC). And, you can buy software from computer stores and advertisers in computer magazines. But there is still a continual need for new, better and creative computer programs.

Is the computer that you plan to buy supported by ample software? Is it compatible with software developed for other computers? A computer store can usually provide better answers to these questions than a department store.

Computer stores are almost always staffed with people who have a fair amount of hardware experience. Many probably built their own personal computer from a kit offered by one of the hobby computer companies. This means that you'll have a much better chance of getting help with requests for "custom" additions or modifications to your machine at a computer store than elsewhere.

For example, say that you want to add plenty of memory to your computer but the original power supply won't handle the extra load. If you don't know anything about power transformers, rectifiers, filter capacitors, and voltage regulators, you're out of luck unless you plan to buy the equipment from a computer store with in-house hardware expertise. For a reasonable fee, many stores will perform the necessary power supply modification and have your machine and its expanded memory up and running in a matter of days.

There are many other hardware services that computer stores will tackle that traditional retailers simply cannot handle. They can add interfacing (things like wires, plugs and sockets) for new peripherals. They can make up cables to connect your computer to other pieces of equipment, and add switches and indicator lights to let you do more things with your machine.

To be sure, most computer shops don't advertise all these extra hardware services. And some are not equipped, willing or able to provide them. But ask around. You'll find that many store owners are willing to do custom hardware work for you and generally for a reasonable fee, particularly if their service technician isn't too busy.

Computer stores generally win hands down when it comes to servicing the machines they sell. Granted, there are some incompetent repair people in every line of business. Nothing beats factory service if you're willing to risk subjecting your precious machine to the perils of shipping and if you are willing to be without it for several weeks or more. So, one of your best service options is the computer store. Often, they can spot a trivial problem like a burned-out power supply capacitor or a broken switch lead in seconds.

Tougher problems take more time, but sometimes they can isolate the difficulty by temporarily replacing a defective circuit board with a good one. This has a fringe benefit for you since the store might let you take your machine back home (with the new board in place) and use it until your own board is repaired. Then you can return to the store and exchange boards.

How do you know that you'll get first class repair service from a computer store? Ask around. Attend some local computer club meetings where you can seek advice. It won't take you long to determine which stores in your area offer the best service.

Once you find a store that has a reputation for good service, be sure to consider buying your machine there, even if the price is slightly higher than by mail order or from a department store. Computer store operators are only human. They'll be much more willing to service machines that they sell than an identical machine you bought from a competitor.

Buying a Used Computer

If you can't afford the price of a new personal computer, why not consider a used machine? Already, many used hobby computers are becoming available for reasonable prices as their owners lose interest in computing or move up to bigger and more powerful machines.

If you want a bargain on a used appliance computer, just be patient. As soon as the owners of Radio Shack TRS-80's and Commodore PET's become addicted to personal computing and decide to move up to a more sophisticated hobby system, you'll find plenty of good buys for appliance machines.

An excellent place to find listings of used personal computers of all kinds is the classified ads of magazines like *BYTE, Interface Age, Kilobaud,* and other hobby computer periodicals.

Another place to find used computers is at computer stores. Some stores might have models that were traded in for newer machines. The store's bulletin board may very well have notices about used computers for sale tucked among the announcements about programming classes and computer club meetings. You can even find used personal computers listed in newspaper want ads. And, computer club members almost always know someone with a system for sale.

If you decide to explore the possibilities of buying a used computer, remember that your chances for warranty protection range from slim to non-existent. Worse, finding someone to service an older, used computer can be a major problem. Keep these negative points in mind. While you might be able to find an excellent used computer bargain, don't set yourself up for major headaches later if you won't be able to have the machine serviced.

Buying Kit Computers

The personal computer began as a hobby-oriented device. You sent a check to MITS, Inc., or one of the other computer kit pioneers and back came a big carton full of circuit boards, switches, a microprocessor chip, and dozens of other electronic parts. The rest was up to you and your soldering iron.

Lear Siegler kit computer.

Today, of course, most personal computers fall in the category of factory-assembled and ready-to-operate appliance machines. But just as some people enjoy building radios and televisions from kits, lots of computer enthusiasts prefer to build their own machines. Besides the challenge of a relatively difficult construction project, the kit builder experiences a well deserved feeling of accomplishment when he turns on his machine for the first time and finds that it really works.

That's not always the way it goes, however! Even the most careful kit builder occasionally makes an error, and finding mistakes can take considerable time. In any event, the end result of building your own computer is a thorough knowledge of how it is put together.

Heathkit's H8 digital computer and H9 video terminal.

That's a major plus, because it means that you might be able to handle most servicing problems should the machine fail to operate. You'll also be in an excellent position to modify and expand your system since you'll have a detailed knowledge of its construction.

Building your own computer might even qualify you for certain educational benefits or credits. The Heath Company, for example, offers a complete line of personal computer kits along with various self-instructional courses in programming. Passing an optional final exam on completion of a course will earn you a certificate of achievement and 3.0 Continuing Education Units (CEUs).

CEUs are a nationally recognized method of certifying completion of non-credit adult education courses. Though CEUs won't earn you a college degree, they can influence some prospective employers. The extension divisions of some 600 colleges, numerous professional associations, and a variety of educational organizations have adopted the CEU method of recognizing non-credit education.

Many hobby computer manufacturers sell computer kits through computer stores and by mail order. If possible, buy your kit from a nearby computer store. This way you'll have access to technical assistance should you run into problems.

Some kits are much easier to assemble than others, so be certain to compare the prospective purchase with your kit building skills. If you've never assembled an electronic kit, you might want to try a simpler kit before tackling a computer.

The Heath Company, for example, sells dozens of different electronic kits. These kits are among the best available and they're supported by excellent assembly manuals. By putting together a digital multimeter, such as Heath's Model IM-1210, you'll gain invaluable kit building experience and end up with a very useful piece of test equipment for troubleshooting the computer and any other electronic kits you plan to build.

Increasing a Computer's Power

COMPUTERS OWNERS like to compare various computers according to their "power." In this context, power isn't a reference to how much electricity a particular computer uses, though more powerful computers usually consume more electrical power than less powerful ones. Instead, power is to a computer what horsepower is to a car. The more there is, the better the performance.

By far the easiest way to increase the power of a computer is to make room for more software. This is accomplished by adding more memory to the machine. More memory means that longer programs can be processed. More memory also means that there is more room to store subroutines, or supplemental programs referred to by a program being processed. Finally, more memory increases the amount of information that can be stored and accessed by a computer in applications like word processing and graphics.

As you may recall, there are several different kinds of computer memories. By definition, every computer includes at least one of them. Even low-cost calculators and video games have solid-state memories that can store hundreds or perhaps thousands of bits of information.

It's relatively easy to add additional memory to most appliance- and hobby-level microcomputers. Often, in fact, memory intended to be added to a computer is considered a computer accessory or peripheral, a topic that is covered in the following chapter. But memories are so important to computers, this entire chapter is devoted to describing the most important memories. First, we'll cover some memory fundamentals that you should know about. Then we'll examine each of the major computer memories and see how they're used with personal computers.

How Memory Increases Computer Power

Before examining the various kinds of computer memories, let's look at some examples of how additional memory increases the power of a computer.

Additional memory means that more program steps can be loaded into a computer. Longer programs are not necessarily more efficient or more important than shorter programs, but all things being equal a long program can include more programming options than a short program. Programming options include features like verbal prompts, or words that the computer flashes on its video screen to ask the operator for new information or instructions during a program.

Programming options also include different ways of writing the same program. The easiest and most obvious way usually takes more memory than the most efficient way. But when your objective is writing a program that works as quickly as possible rather than taking lots of time to write the most efficient program possible, added memory space becomes a real bonus.

More memory makes it easier to store more than one program in a computer. You can always save programs by writing them on paper, but typing them into a computer every time they're needed is time-consuming. Storing programs in a memory directly accessible to a computer is much more efficient. It also means a program can refer to one or more other programs as subroutines.

Computers make ideal electronic file cabinets for storing, organizing, and retrieving recipes, school records, small business inventories, household budget figures, tax records, and names, addresses and telephone numbers. Many of these applications make little or no use of the computer's immense computational ability, but all of them depend on the computer's ability to organize and sort information, and to store the information in and retrieve it from a memory. The more memory that's available, the bigger the capacity of the electronic file cabinet.

Many personal computers can be used to produce images on the screen of a video display. This feature is often called video graphics since its original application was producing various kinds of charts and graphs on a computer's screen. This application is still very important. But personal computer users have found many other uses for graphics.

The graphics feature is ideal for playing games. Players, cards, balls, spaceships, goal lines, and other objects can be electronically painted on and erased from the screen. As you might expect, however, the more elaborate the picture, the more memory that's required. Some computers with lots of memory can produce very detailed video pictures; others are limited to relatively coarse, low-resolution pictures.

Using a computer to remember and edit words typed

into a keyboard is called word processing. Personal computer owners who are fortunate enough to have a printer connected to their computer have the nucleus of a basic word-processing system.

Since the computer interprets the characters typed into the keyboard and places them in the memory, it's possible to manipulate the information being typed with software. One kind of word-processing software, for instance, arranges the information so that it is printed out justified, or flush on both the left and right margins. Other software for word processing allows the mass production of letters, greeting cards, sales proposals, advertising brochures, and other printed matter in a personalized manner.

Word processing, for obvious reasons, requires plenty of memory, but it's certain to become one of the most popular applications for personal computers. Already many computer hobbyists are using their machines for word-processing applications ranging from automatic preparation of Christmas cards to various money-making enterprises.

Adding, or at least being able to add, more memory to a computer means that you'll be able to expand the power and capabilities of the computer at some future time. This means that you'll be able to use a personal computer for completely new applications like electronic mail, continuing education, and the home office.

How Words, Symbols, and Characters Are Stored

How electronic circuits can process, organize, and sort ordinary decimal numbers if the numbers are first converted into the two-digit or bit binary number system has been discussed. It's easy for computer memories to store numbers by representing the binary bit "1" with a transistor that's turned on, or by a tiny magnetic field on a piece of recording tape. Similarly, the binary bit "0" can be represented by a transistor that's been turned off, or by the absence of a magnetic field on a

The ASCII Code

BIT NUMBERS												
						0	0	0	0	1	1	1	1
						0	0	1	1	0	0	1	1
						0	1	0	1	0	1	0	1
b7 b6 b5	b4	b3	b2	b1	COLUMN →	0	1	2	3	4	5	6	7
↓ ↓ ↓	↓	↓	↓	↓	ROW ↓								
	0	0	0	0	0	NUL	DLE	SP	0	@	P		p
	0	0	0	1	1	SOH	DC1	!	1	A	Q	a	q
	0	0	1	0	2	STX	DC2	‖	2	B	R	b	r
	0	0	1	1	3	ETX	DC3	#	3	C	S	c	s
	0	1	0	0	4	EOT	DC4	$	4	D	T	d	t
	0	1	0	1	5	ENQ	NAK	%	5	E	U	e	u
	0	1	1	0	6	ACK	SYN	&	6	F	V	f	v
	0	1	1	1	7	BEL	ETB	'	7	G	W	g	w
	1	0	0	0	8	BS	CAN	(	8	H	X	h	x
	1	0	0	1	9	HT	EM	)	9	I	Y	i	y
	1	0	1	0	A	LF	SUB	*	:	J	Z	j	z
	1	0	1	1	b	VT	ESC	+	;	K	[	k	{
	1	1	0	0	C	FF	FS	,	<	L	\	l	¦
	1	1	0	1	d	CR	GS	–	=	M	]	m	}
	1	1	1	0	E	SO	RS	.	>	N	∴	n	~
	1	1	1	1	F	SI	US	/	?	O	¯	o	DEL

Examples: The ASCII Code for the letter W is 1010111. The code for the ? is 0111111.

The American Standard Code For Information Interchange (ASCII) is used by almost all personal computers.

tape. But how does a computer remember characters like letters of the alphabet, symbols like punctuation marks, and entire words and sentences? The easiest way is to assign each character or symbol its own binary number or code. The computer can interpret a binary number as strictly a number, or it can interpret the number as a character or symbol.

The most common character and symbol code used in personal computers is ASCII (pronounced "as-ski"). ASCII is an acronym for American Standard Code for Information Interchange.

Don't worry if you think that you have to memorize any or all of the ASCII code to use a personal computer. You don't have to know the ASCII code to make effective use of a computer, but it's a good idea to at least see how the code is organized. This will give you an intuitive feel for how computer memories store information, and that will make your computer seem a little less intimidating when it snaps back at you with various orders and requests on its video display.

Types of Computer Memories

There are two main types of computer memories, read-only and read-write.

Read-only memories contain permanent or semipermanent information that can be read by a computer when it is ordered to perform some specific operation. The information may be in the form of programs or tables of information. Think of it as a computer's internal operating instructions.

Read-write memories are designed to store temporary information such as programs typed into a computer's keyboard, results of software operations, and lists of information. You can think of a read-write memory as a computer's erasable scratch pad. Information on the scratch pad may be saved for only a few thousandths of a second, then erased, and replaced by new information. Or, the information may be saved indefinitely.

Both read-only and read-write memories come in many different configurations, ranging from magnetic tape to various kinds of solid-state integrated circuits. The simplest way to learn about the various kinds of read-only and read-write memories is to lump all of them into two categories: memories with and memories without moving parts.

Examples of memories with moving parts include tape recorders and magnetic disks. Both of these memories are called mass storage devices since they can store huge quantities of information. They are fairly large and relatively slow when compared to memories without moving parts. They also pose more of a maintenance problem.

Memories without moving parts include semiconductor arrays and other solid-state devices. The importance of these memories lies in their small size and very rapid speed. These advantages are expensive, however, since it costs far more to store a bit of information in a memory without moving parts than in one with moving parts.

You'll probably use both kinds of memories if you buy your own computer, so be sure to read the rest of this chapter carefully because the cost of adding memory to your computer can easily exceed the cost of the computer!

Memories with Moving Parts

There are several kinds of computer memories with moving parts, but personal computers make almost exclusive use of only two—the cassette recorder and the floppy disk. Both of these memories store information in the form of tiny magnetized spots on ordinary recording tape or plastic disks coated with the same substance used to make recording tape. Since both of these memories offer a relatively cheap way of storing large quantities of information, you should know something about how they work and be familiar with the advantages and disadvantages of each.

Cassette Recorder Memories

More than likely you already own a cassette recorder suitable for use as either a read-only or read-write memory with most appliance- and hobby-level personal computers. Cassette tape is not the most efficient way to store large quantities of computer data, but for now it's certainly the cheapest. Considering the high cost of more advanced memories, several of which we'll be covering later in this chapter, it makes sense to devote a fair amount of space to cassette tape as a computer memory medium.

In principle, storing information on magnetic tape is as simple as magnetizing a steel needle by stroking it with a magnet. Recording tape is made from a tough plastic film coated on one side with a thin layer of an easily magnetized substance like iron oxide. You can store a bit of information on a piece of recording tape by placing an ordinary magnet near the tape's iron oxide surface.

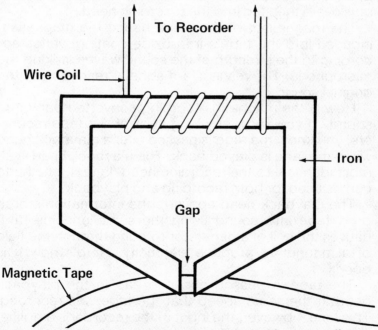

Information is recorded on magnetic tape by a recording head made from iron and wrapped with a coil of wire.

Recording machines use a special electromagnet called a recording head to store information on tape. A recording head is little more than an iron form wrapped with several layers of wire. If electricity is allowed to flow through the coil, the iron becomes magnetic. Up to a point, the magnetism becomes stronger as more electricity is allowed to flow through the coil. Remove the electricity and the iron loses its magnetic properties.

A sound tape recording is made by passing the recording tape in a reel or cassette over a thin gap in the recording head. The gap concentrates the head's magnetic field into a very small area of the tape. Music or speech entering a microphone is converted into electricity and boosted in strength by an amplifier. The beefed-up electrical signals, that retain all of the frequency and amplitude variations of the original voice or music, are then fed into the recording head.

The magnetism of the head, hence the magnetism induced into the tape's iron oxide coating, varies according to the strength of the sound waves striking the microphone. The result is a magnetic recording of the original sound.

How is the magnetic recording converted back into sound? If you know anything at all about tape recorders, you know the tape is passed over a playback head when the tape is played back. The playback head is almost identical to the recording head. In fact, one head can be used for both recording and playback.

The playback head converts the information stored on a tape into sound using the same principle that causes the coil of a generator rotating through the field of a magnet to produce electricity. Here's how it is done:

The tape is passed over the gap in the playback head at the same speed that the tape was recorded. This time, however, the input of the recorder's amplifier is connected to the playback head instead of a microphone. As the magnetized regions on the tape pass by the gap in the head, they induce tiny electrical currents in the head's coil. The currents are much too feeble to power a speaker, but the amplifier easily boosts them up to the necessary level. The result is a reasonably faithful reproduction of the original sound that entered the microphone when the recording was made.

The recording is only reasonably faithful because of a couple of characteristics common to both speech and music. The intensity of both varies from the quietest whisper to the loudest clash of a cymbal. And the frequency of both can range from the snap of a finger to the clear high pitch of a flute.

This wide variation of sound amplitude and frequency places difficult technical constraints on tape recording equipment, as audiophiles already know. A truly perfect recording is impossible to achieve because of slight variations in recording and playback speeds, unwanted electrical noise created in the amplifier and microphone, and imperfect response of both the microphone and amplifier to various sound frequencies.

By now you're probably wondering why we've spent so much time reviewing how a tape recorder records—and plays back—speech and music when the subject at hand is storing computer information. The reason is that understanding some of the subtleties of sound recording will help you understand more about the recording of computer data.

Digital information is much simpler than the complex audio signals of music and speech. This means that almost any tape recorder of reasonable quality can be used as a mass-data storage memory for a personal computer.

The key to the ease with which computer data can be stored on magnetic tape is the binary or two-state nature of the data. Instead of being required to faithfully record an immense range of sound intensities and frequencies, the tape need only record the simple absence (binary "0") or presence (binary "1") of an electrical signal.

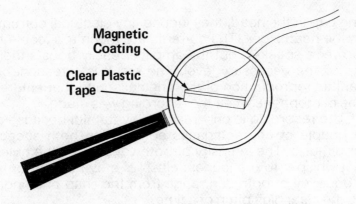

Magnetic Coating

Clear Plastic Tape

Magnetic recording tape is simply clear plastic tape with a magnetic coating.

How are "0's" and "1's" recorded on tape? There are several ways.

The first is simply to magnetize small spaces on the tape where "1's" are stored and not magnetize areas where "0's" are stored. This method can store lots of binary bits in a very limited area. But it's subject to missed or dropped bits. These are errors that sometimes occur when a bit is not recorded or when a tape is played back and a bit is not read out, owing to the uneven spread of magnetizable oxide on the tape. A single dropped bit can cause an entire computer program to fail. That is why it's important to use good quality recording tape when recording computer data. The recorder's frequency response and the record and playback speeds of the recorder are not nearly as critical as when speech or music is recorded.

The second method is more complicated but very reliable because binary "0's" and "1's" are recorded on tape as musical tones. One very popular tone method of data recording is known by the rather improbable name of Kansas City Standard after the city where a

Magnetized Regions

Magnetic Tape

The simplest way to store computer data on tape is to let magnetized spots correspond to 1's and nonmagnetized spots to 0's.

group of computer hobbyists agreed on its specifications in 1975. With this system, "0's" are stored as a brief burst of tone with a frequency of 1200 Hertz (one Hertz or Hz is equivalent to one cycle per second). And, "1's" are stored as a burst of tone with a frequency of 2400 Hz.

Another tone method of data recording is used by the KIM-1 computer made by MOS Technology, an economical and very popular hobby microcomputer. KIM stores both "0's" and "1's" in a burst of tone lasting only 0.007452 second. The tone begins with a frequency of 3700 Hz for both "0's" and "1's." The tone is changed to 2400 Hz two-thirds of the way through the tonal burst to indicate a "0." A "1" is indicated by switching to 2400 Hz one-third of the way through the burst.

Why cover all the various methods for recording computer data in such detail? Though you need not understand how computer data is stored on magnetic tape to use a computer or even to store data on cassette tapes, it is important to know that different computers often use very different methods of recording data. A tape containing a program that was recorded using the Kansas City Standard would be ignored by a KIM-1 microcomputer since the KIM uses a totally different method of data recording. Although the Kansas

City system is widely used, it is the slowest cassette tape method. And you'd be surprised at how impatient one can be when it takes five minutes to dump an entire file as compared to three minutes with another system. Therefore, it's important to know something about how your computer records data on tape if you plan to store programs and other information on cassettes.

Will you be able to obtain a range of software tapes from more than one company? Will you be able to exchange tapes containing data and programs with your friends and associates? If the answer to these questions is no, is there a reliable interface circuit that will permit your computer to communicate with someone else's, even though they use different methods for storing data? If the answer to this question is yes, the question of which computer to buy is not nearly as limited as it might otherwise be. Moreover, this versatility may not even be important to you.

Some Tips About Tapes

When recording computer data with a cassette recorder, it's important to remember that tape quality is usually more important than the quality of the recorder. This is because the magnetic coating applied to recording tape can have soft spots where the coating is very thin or has been rubbed off. These spots may not record data properly. Since a single lost bit can ruin an entire program, it's important to use premium tape.

Most computer programs can be recorded on only a few minutes of tape. Radio Shack's TRS-80, for example, can dump the entire contents of its semiconductor read-write memory in less than five minutes. For this reason, Radio Shack sells a C-10 cassette that holds up to five minutes of data on each side of the tape. The company recommends that a single program be stored on each side of a short tape rather than attempting to save several programs on a long tape.

This procedure simplifies matters when it's time to load a program stored on a tape into a computer since it's not necessary to find the point where one program ends and another begins. That can be difficult to do since the human ear cannot understand the strange sounds of computer data recorded on a cassette.

There is, however, a relatively simple way to use a long tape to record a series of programs. All that's necessary is to insert a few words of verbal introduction immediately prior to each program. The recorder's counter is then used to keep track of each program's approximate location. It's necessary to listen to the tape before connecting the recorder to the computer, but this method does allow you to store more than one program on each side of a cassette.

Whichever method one uses to record programs on cassette tape, it's important to remember that even the highest quality cassette recorders and tapes are vulnerable to several potential problems when pressed into service as computer memories. Here are five tips to keep in mind:

1. It's important to use caution when attempting to record computer data on a tape that already contains, or has previously contained, computer data. The recorder might not erase the old data completely when the new data is recorded. This might cause the computer to read both new and old information when the tape is read. The result is mass confusion.

Another problem when recording on tapes that have been previously-used is what happens to the end of a long program left on the tape after a short, new program is recorded. The computer might load your new program as well as what's left of the old one! Again, the result can be very confusing.

2. It's extremely important not to lose even a single bit of information stored on a computer tape. Therefore, tapes should be kept away from anything that has magnetic properties such as AC motors, power supplies, and magnets.

3. Avoid using tapes with leaders when recording computer data. A leader is a length of tape without a magnetic coating. It's usually placed at one or both ends of standard recording tape. Unless you make sure that the leader is out of the way (or use a tape without a leader), the computer may try to dump data onto or read data from the leader. This means incomplete program storage or loading.

4. Should you decide to acquire your own computer, don't attempt to use a cassette recorder to save an elaborate program that you've composed at the keyboard until you've practiced saving and reloading a few simple programs first. More than one enthusiastic novice has accidentally lost a newly-composed program by failing to record it on tape properly.

5. Finally, the manufacturers of various computers usually provide detailed instructions about how to use a cassette recorder with their equipment. Be sure to familiarize yourself with these instructions before you make a purchasing decision. If you plan to record plenty of programs and data on cassette tape, you'll want an efficient data storage procedure. A procedure that requires you to push buttons and adjust controls every time you want to read out or save some data might be inexpensive, but it will use up lots of time.

Before cassette tapes became popular for storing computer data, paper tape was the only low-cost medium for bulk information storage. Holes punched on tape represent characters. When the paper tape runs through a tape-reader machine, the presence or absence of a hole is detected and transmitted in code to the computer. A paper-tape punch is needed to "record." Reader and punch are often combined. This system's greatest use is with Teletype printing terminals. Many hobbyists bought used Teletype machines that include this feature.

As a bulk storage medium, paper tape has fallen into disfavor because, though cheap, the write/read speed is very slow compared to cassette tape. About 10 times as long, in fact. Moreover, large quantities of paper tape are needed as compared to cassette tape.

The Disk Memory

Disk memory systems are much faster and easier to use than cassette recorders. They're also much more expensive. A disk memory system can easily cost as much as or even more than a complete personal computer system!

As explained earlier, a disk memory system stores information by magnetizing small spots on the surface of a metal or plastic disk that is similar in appearance to a phonograph record.

Plastic disks are coated with the same kind of magnetic material used to make recording tape. They're usually called flexible or floppy disks to distinguish

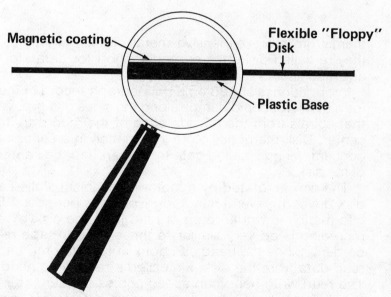

Disk memories store data on the magnetic surface of a plastic or metal disk that looks like a 45 rpm record.

Here is a floppy disk in its protective envelope.

them from more expensive metal disks. Sometimes, they're called diskettes or media (short for data storage medium).

Information is stored on a phonograph record in the form of microscopic bumps along the sides of a groove that spirals from the outside edge of the record to its center. Disk memories store information in a series of concentric rings, called data tracks, around the center of the disk.

The disk is rotated by a motor mechanism, called a disk drive, at several hundred revolutions per second. Information is written onto or read from the disk by a recording head very similar to those used in tape recorders. Since the head can both write data onto and read data from the disk, it's called a read-write head. The read-write head can speed across the surface of the disk to any of a hundred or more data tracks in a fraction of a second.

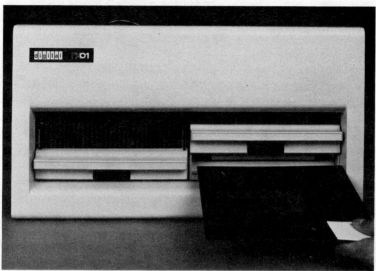
This is how a floppy is inserted into a disk memory system.

A typical floppy disk system can store a quarter million bytes of information on a 6.5-inch diameter floppy. And, it can retrieve this information quickly with the help of a precision mechanism that can propel the read-write head to any of its data tracks within three-tenths of a second. All of the information stored on the disk can be read out in less than a second!

The total information storage capacity of a disk is determined both by the size of the disk and the precision of the drive mechanism. Some disk systems record data on both sides of the medium to double its storage capacity.

Due to the high price of disk memories, there's been a trend to a compact diskette system called the mini-floppy. Minifloppies measure only 5-1/4 inches in diameter, and a typical minifloppy diskette can store about 100,000 bytes. Minifloppy systems are made by several personal computer companies.

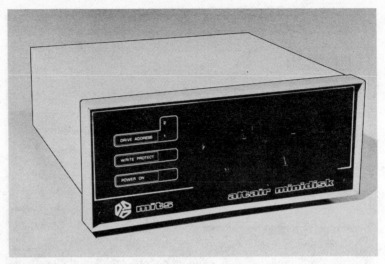

This ALTAIR Minidisk System, made by Pertec Computer Corp., is designed to store more than 71,000 bytes per floppy.

How does the computer know where information is stored on a floppy? Two ways are available, both of which keep track of information according to the data track that it's stored on and the position of the information on the track. A disk has a fixed number of data tracks so that it's relatively easy to keep tabs on which track a specific program or chunk of data is located. But where the information is located on the track is a more difficult problem.

The problem, however, is solved by dividing the disk into sectors much as a pie is cut into wedges. A disk may be divided into 2, 4, 8, 16, 32 or more sectors (or slices) by placing a ring of small index holes near the center of the disk. Each hole indicates a sector. A light beam detects the holes as they sweep by and keeps the computer informed about which sector is passing by the read-write head at any given instant.

This method of dividing a disk into sectors with the

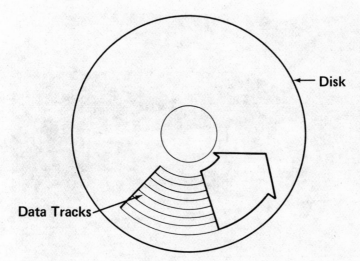

Disk

Data Tracks

Information is stored on a disk along concentric rings called data tracks.

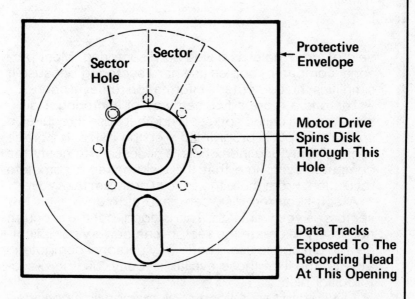

Protective Envelope

Sector

Sector Hole

Motor Drive Spins Disk Through This Hole

Data Tracks Exposed To The Recording Head At This Opening

A floppy disk is divided into sectors with the help of small holes around the center hole.

Up to 600,000 bytes can be stored on each of the two floppies that can be simultaneously inserted into this system.

help of index holes is called hard sectoring. Most personal computer floppies use hard sectoring because it simplifies the computer's information retrieval chores.

There is a more advanced way of sectoring a disk, however. It's called soft sectoring because it requires a special computer program to slice the disk into storage sectors. Only one index hole is necessary to notify the computer each time that the disk makes a complete revolution. From there the special program takes over.

A soft-sectored disk can have as many or as few sectors as you want it to. This is good, but the program necessary to create the sectors can be very complicated and difficult to use. That's why personal computers, at least most of those available today, use hard-sectored floppies.

As you can see, a floppy disk memory is a considerably more sophisticated data storage system than a cassette recorder. With a suitable disk memory system, you can save programs and any other information typed into your computer (addresses, dates, phone numbers, bank balance, etc.) in fractions of a second. And, you can load information from a disk into your computer just as quickly.

Contrast this with the cassette tape recorder. The computer-disk combination is almost fully automated, but you must operate various switches and controls to use a cassette recorder with a computer. That can be time-consuming and prone to error. Cost, of course, is the bottom line for many personal computer enthusiasts. For most, the $500 to $1500 price of a personal computer disk memory system is simply too expensive.

On the bright side, disk memories sold for a minimum of $10,000 a few short years ago, so today's prices are actually a bargain. Prices for disk memories, particularly the minifloppy variety, are expected to continue to drop, so it's important to stay informed about the market. You might even find a good buy in a used disk memory. This is particularly true now since many businesses are updating their computer systems to keep up with the latest technological advances.

Memories Without Moving Parts

Solid-state memories without moving parts are semiconductor circuits made by using the same integrated circuit technology responsible for the microprocessor. These memories are an essential part of every computer. They're not used for bulk or mass storage, however, due to high cost. That's the province of a floppy disk or a cassette tape.

Until recently, solid-state memories were very expensive. As semiconductor firms gained more experience in manufacturing intricate microprocessor and memory chips, prices for both components dropped considerably. Today, semiconductor memories that can store thousands of bits of information in a space smaller than this letter "o" are available for less than a penny per bit. This is still much higher in cost than disk or tape.

Two types of semiconductor solid-state memories are used in personal computers (and programmable calculators, too). They are called ROMs and RAMs.

ROM means read-only memory and RAM means random-access memory. Actually, both ROMs and RAMs are random-access memories, so let's find out something about random access as it applies to semiconductor memories. Then, we'll see how ROMs and RAMs are used to store computer data.

Random-Access Semiconductor Memories

Both cassette tape and disk memories are "serial-access" memories because a length of tape or a data track on a disk must be searched to find a particular piece of information. Disk memories are faster and more efficient than tapes since only one of a hundred or more data tracks has to be searched.

Random access means a bit (or byte) of information stored in a memory can be retrieved (or stored) just as fast as any other bit. All that's necessary is to supply the location, or address in computer jargon, of the bit, and the "0" or "1" stored there is quickly made available within a fixed time interval (the access time).

Air-Line Distances Between Six Selected Cities

	Lima	Paris	Tokyo	Cairo	Rome	New York
Lima	—	6370	9631	7726	6750	3639
Paris	6370	—	6053	1998	690	3636
Tokyo	9631	6053	—	5958	6142	6757
Cairo	7726	1998	5958	—	1326	5619
Rome	6750	690	6142	1326	—	4293
New York	3639	3636	6757	5619	4293	—

Figure 1

Random access is much faster and more efficient than serial access. An everyday example of random access is a table like the accompanying one showing airline distances (Figure 1).

Figure 2 shows how you would use the table to quickly find the distance from Tokyo to Rome. Thanks

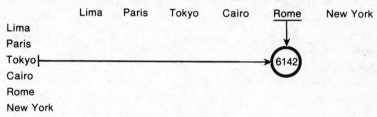

Air Line Distances Between Six Selected Cities

	Lima	Paris	Tokyo	Cairo	Rome	New York
Lima						
Paris						
Tokyo					6142	
Cairo						
Rome						
New York						

Figure 2

to the random accessibility of information in the table, the distance between any two of the given cities can be found in approximately the same time.

Figure 3 shows a serial version of the random-access table. Organizing the information in the table in serial fashion, as on a cassette tape, increases the amount of time necessary to find the distance between two cities.

A simple analogy to a disk memory can be established by dividing the table in Figure 3 into six divisions (Lima—Lima through Lima—New York; Paris—Lima through Paris—New York; etc.). Each division is then considered a data track on a disk. The disk memory's read-write head can reduce the time required to find the distance between two cities by jumping to the track designated by the first city in a given pair and then scanning only the six pairs on that track.

A cassette tape version of the table is not so efficient. It must scan one pair of cities at a time until the specified pair is found. If that pair happens to be New York—Rome, the read-write head will have to scan 35

Air-Line Distances Between Six Selected Cities

Cities	Distance
Lima — Lima	—
Lima — Paris	6370
Lima — Tokyo	9631
Lima — Cairo	7726
Lima — Rome	6750
Lima — New York	3639
Paris — Lima	6370
Paris — Paris	—
Paris — Tokyo	6053
Paris — Cairo	1998
Paris — Rome	690
Paris — New York	3636
Tokyo — Lima	9631
Tokyo — Paris	6053
Tokyo — Tokyo	—
Tokyo — Cairo	5958
Tokyo — Rome	6142
Tokyo — New York	6757
Cairo — Lima	7726
Cairo — Paris	1998
Cairo — Tokyo	5958
Cairo — Cairo	—
Cairo — Rome	1326
Cairo — New York	5619
Rome — Lima	6750
Rome — Paris	690
Rome — Tokyo	6142
Rome — Cairo	1326
Rome — Rome	—
Rome — New York	4293
New York — Lima	3639
New York — Paris	3636
New York — Tokyo	6757
New York — Cairo	5619
New York — Rome	4293
New York — New York	—

Figure 3

pairs of cities before arriving at the requested mileage figure.

How Information Is Organized in ROMs and RAMs

Earlier, we learned how information in most personal computers is processed as 8-bit binary numbers called words or bytes. These binary numbers can symbolize decimal numbers or letters of the alphabet, punctuation marks, and other characters. Hence, calling them words or bytes instead of numbers makes sense.

The storage capacity of the ROM and RAM memories used in microcomputers is specified according to the number of bytes or words that the memory can store. Byte is almost always used to indicate a word having eight bits. Many microcomputers being designed for the next generation of personal computers

This circuit board, which can be plugged into a small computer, contains 48 memory integrated circuits.

will process two bytes at one time. Memories for these machines will be organized in either 8-bit bytes or 16-bit words.

The information storage capacity of ROMs and RAMs is considerably higher today than only a few years ago. Several semiconductor firms are now making silicon memory chips that can store more than 64,000 bits of information! These chips, however, are very expensive since their complexity and their comparatively large size result in a relatively low production yield. In other words, it's possible to make many more small storage capacity memory chips than high capacity chips during the same production run. For this reason, semiconductor memories for personal computers are usually made by combining a number of small- to moderate-capacity memory chips on a circuit board.

A typical personal computer may include 4096 bytes of memory made from 32 memory chips that are capable of storing 1024 bits each, or eight chips capable of

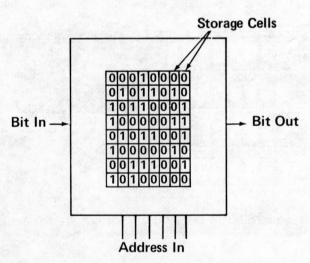

Each storage cell in a solid-state memory has its own binary address.

storing 4096 bits each. These chips are usually organized as an array of individual memory cells. A bit can be stored in or retrieved from a particular cell by applying the binary address for the cell to the chip's address inputs.

Multiple-bit words or bytes are stored by arranging a number of chips so that each contributes one bit to the stored word. All the address inputs are tied together so that a single address accesses a word having as many bits as the number of chips in the memory.

You might be wondering why semiconductor memories store odd numbers of bits (like 1024 and 4096) instead of nice round numbers (like 1000 and 4000). This is because the total storage capacity of a memory is determined by the number of address connections available. The addresses are given in binary and are multiples of power of two (1, 2, 4, 8, 16, 32, etc.), hence the rather unusual numbers for a memory's maximum storage capacity. The highest address for a memory

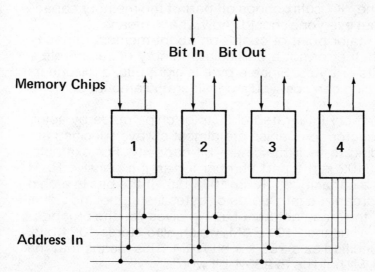

Here is how several memory integrated circuits are connected together to increase the number of bits that can be stored.

with eight address connections, for example, is 11111111 in binary. This is equivalent to 255 in decimal which means 256 memory cells can be accessed. The extra cell is at address 00000000.

Figure 4 shows the relationship between the number of address connections available, the highest possible binary address, and the total number of storage locations that can be accessed. Fortunately, you don't have to memorize this table to understand all you need to know about semiconductor memories! Computer designers have selected several key memory storage capacities and developed a simple way of designating them with the unit Kilobyte (K).

The ones that you should know about are those from 1024 to 65,536. And the shortcut way of designating them is to drop the last three digits and replace them with a "K." Thus, a 1024-bit ROM is called a 1K ROM. Likewise, a 16,384-bit RAM is called a 16K RAM. The "K" comes from a Greek prefix meaning thousand. Using the "K" suffix chops off part of the memory capacity, but everyone should know what it means.

A major point of confusion about memory capacity is whether or not a particular memory capacity refers to bits or bytes. Since a byte is eight bits, a misunderstanding can cost you a considerable amount of memory!

Memory integrated circuits or chips made by semiconductor companies are almost always specified according to their maximum bit capacity. For example, the 2102 is the part number for an inexpensive RAM with a capacity of 1K, or 1024 bits. If the bits in a chip are organized into words or bytes instead of individual bits, the manufacturer of a chip gives you the organization. Thus the 2101 RAM, which also stores 1024 bits, is specified as a 256 x 4 bit RAM. This means that the chip will hold up to 256 4-bit words.

Memories made from individual integrated circuits by personal computer makers are not always specified with such precision. Indeed, it's almost standard for a

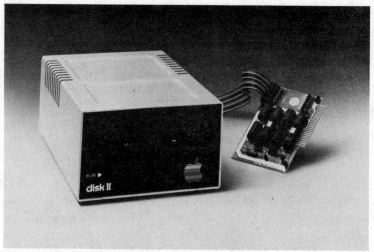

Apple Computer's Disk II floppy system.

Number of Address Bits (in decimal)	Highest Address (in binary)	Total Number of Addresses (in decimal)
1	1	2
2	1 1	4
3	1 1 1	8
4	1 1 1 1	16
5	1 1 1 1 1	32
6	1 1 1 1 1 1	64
7	1 1 1 1 1 1 1	128
8	1 1 1 1 1 1 1 1	256
9	1 1 1 1 1 1 1 1 1	512
10	1 1 1 1 1 1 1 1 1 1	1,024
11	1 1 1 1 1 1 1 1 1 1 1	2,048
12	1 1 1 1 1 1 1 1 1 1 1 1	4,096
13	1 1 1 1 1 1 1 1 1 1 1 1 1	8,192
14	1 1 1 1 1 1 1 1 1 1 1 1 1 1	16,384
15	1 1 1 1 1 1 1 1 1 1 1 1 1 1 1	32,768
16	1 1 1 1 1 1 1 1 1 1 1 1 1 1 1 1	65,536

Figure 4

computer company to call a memory with a storage capacity of 4096 8-bit bytes a 4K memory. The reason for this is the almost universal use of 8-bit microcomputers. When 16-bit microcomputers become more common, memories will probably be specified more accurately. Until then, be sure to ask whether that 8K memory that you're planning to buy holds 8K bytes or 8K bits.

Read-Only Memories (ROMs)

There are two kinds of ROMs, and both are designed to permanently remember a fixed set of numbers, data, computer instructions or even complete computer programs.

A factory or mask-programmable ROM receives the information that it's been assigned to remember when manufactured. The other kind of ROM is called a field-programmable ROM or PROM. As its name implies, a PROM can be programmed or loaded with information by its user. Once loaded, the information cannot be erased.

Both kinds of ROMs are very important to personal computers. Factory-programmed ROMs are particularly important. Consider the BASIC language capability that is now commonly available as a built-in feature of many personal computers. Until recently, the only way to communicate with personal computers in a higher-level language like BASIC was to load a complicated program called an interpreter into the computer's RAM memory. The interpreter responds to commands typed into the computer's keyboard by ordering the machine's microprocessor to perform various sequences of operations.

BASIC interpreters are available on cassette tape or perforated paper tape, but loading them into a computer's memory is time consuming. And there's always the possibility of dropping a bit and having to repeat the entire loading procedure. Worse, it's necessary to give up a big chunk of the computer's main solid-state memory to hold the BASIC interpreter. It means that you can't turn the machine off if you don't want to lose the BASIC interpreter.

All these problems are solved with the help of a ROM or PROM that has been loaded with the BASIC interpreter. The ROM can be plugged directly into the computer's main circuit board where it immediately goes into action when the computer is turned on. ROMs or PROMs with interpreters for different BASIC dialects or entirely different languages can also be used.

ROMs have many applications in addition to the one that we've been considering. Remember the explanations of how calculators and computers operate? The built-in memory that tells a calculator how to add a couple of numbers together is a ROM imprinted on the silicon chip alongside the calculator's control, arithmetic, and register circuits.

Similarly, the microinstructions that tell a computer how to branch from one part of a program to another, or to add two numbers are contained in a ROM. Like the calculator chip, the computer's microinstruction ROM is often located on the microprocessor chip that forms the electronic brain of the computer.

ROMs are also used to decode computer information. To decode is to convert binary information into some other format such as decimal numbers that people can understand. Calculators use a ROM to decode binary information into electrical signals that turn on the segments in each of the digits in the calculator's readout. This allows the calculator to solve problems using the number system that it understands, while giving you the results in a number system that you understand.

Before moving on to RAMs, let's take time to introduce the PROM in a little more detail. Those who are interested in hobby computers should definitely make an effort to learn more about PROMs because they provide a unique way of increasing a computer's power.

Appliance-grade computer users may also find PROMs to be an important tool.

How do PROMs increase computer power? There are many possibilities, but let's consider one that was briefly mentioned earlier: advanced programming languages. We've already seen how many personal computers are given a BASIC language capability thanks to an interpreter stored in a factory-programmed ROM. Other languages can be placed on ROMs as well. But making a ROM is an expensive process. A company might have to order several thousand or more just to get the price for each ROM down to a level where it can be included in a computer. That means custom languages, or languages that are used by only a limited number of customers are out.

Enter the relatively inexpensive PROM that can be quickly and reliably programmed by the computer maker with a PROM programmer. Computer hobbyists sometimes build their own programmers or load information and programs into the PROM a bit at a time with an ordinary power supply.

This means that a computer company or even an independent computer store can afford to offer customized languages or special programs for various computers without the expense of producing a large number of factory-programmed ROMs. The PROM is simply plugged into a special socket in the computer. It can be replaced with a different PROM for another short, frequently used computer language much more quickly and conveniently than by loading the new information from a cassette tape or floppy disk. And, there's no risk of dropping a bit and no tie-up of the computer's main read-write memory.

Incidentally, in case you're wondering how information is loaded into a PROM, the process is really very simple. The PROM is shipped from the factory with a ''0'' stored in each of its memory locations. Each ''0'' is connected to an aluminum grid inside the PROM with a very short length of nichrome, which is the wire used in toasters and glows red-hot when you're burning some toast. It becomes hot because it tends to resist the flow of electricity.

A PROM is programmed by causing electricity to flow through each memory cell where a "1" is desired. This heats and, within a few thousandths of a second, melts the nichrome. The result is a "1" entered into the PROM.

The programming process is continued a bit at a time until the entire memory is loaded. Unlike tape or disk, the program cannot be erased and a new one inserted. There are some ROMs where this is possible, though, called erasable ROMs or EPROMs.

Since the PROM becomes rather warm while it's being programmed, computer people often refer to this programming procedure as burning a PROM. Don't confuse this with another common computer phrase that refers to burned-in memories, circuits, computers, etc. A burned-in circuit or memory is simply a piece of equipment that's been operated for some specified time period before it is sold. This allows potential problems to be detected before the equipment leaves the factory.

Read-Write Memories (RAMs)

RAMs, like cassette tapes and floppy disks, are read-write memories. Since they're solid-state integrated circuits, they operate at much faster speeds than tapes and floppies and have no mechanical maintenance problems. But the cost of storing a bit in a RAM is much more than saving the bit on tape or a floppy.

A typical large-capacity RAM memory board designed to be plugged into a computer costs approximately 2.35 cents per 8-bit byte or about three-tenths of a cent per bit. This sounds cheap, and it is when compared to RAM prices several years ago, but a bit can be stored on cassette tape for a lot less. Indeed, a few inches of tape can store hundreds or even thousands of bits.

This RAM circuit board can store up to 16,384 bytes or 131,072 bits in 48 integrated circuits.

RAMs are either static or dynamic. Static RAMs save the information that they contain as long as power is supplied. Dynamic RAMs can store information for only a few thousandths of a second, however. They require special circuits to "refresh" the information stored in the memory.

A problem with most kinds of RAMs is volatility. Data stored in a ROM is permanent. It does not require electricity to retain information. Turn off the power to a RAM, however, and its contents are lost. This can be a major nuisance, especially if a power failure occurs after you've spent hours at the keyboard of a computer composing an elaborate program.

A new kind of RAM that uses very little power may eventually solve the volatility problem. It's called the CMOS (Complementary Metal-Oxide-Silicon) RAM. You'll hear more about it in the future. CMOS RAMs can operate for days on the power of a couple of flashlight batteries! Already, several calculators with continuous CMOS memories are available. When the calculator is turned off, a small trickle of electrical current from its batteries preserves the information in the RAM.

Until low-power RAMs are available, personal computer owners will have to use precautions whenever loading programs into their machines. There's nothing more frustrating than spending 30 minutes loading a fancy program and then having to turn off the machine for the night when you don't have a method of saving the program on cassette tape or a floppy disk.

Despite its drawbacks, adding more RAM to a computer is one of the most effective ways of increasing its power. A floppy system can hold 100,000 or more bytes per disk, but transferring information between the disk and the computer is much slower than when all the information is stored in a RAM.

For relatively simple computer applications neither additional RAM nor a floppy system may be necessary. But for more advanced systems where rapid program execution is imperative, the RAM is superior to the floppy.

How To Buy More RAM

Let's assume that you own an appliance-grade personal computer that was supplied with 4K of factory-installed RAM. You want to add another 4K of RAM so that you can store longer programs. Let's further assume that both the manufacturer of your computer and a small peripheral company make 4K memories that will fit your computer. While the small company's product is cheaper, you don't know if it's as reliable as the memory made by the computer company. What do you do?

This question, and it's a difficult one, has been faced by almost every home computerist since the MITS ALTAIR was introduced in 1975. Because of the large number of small companies that made add-on memory boards, it is extremely difficult to make specific recommendations about particular products. Some general guidelines, however, can be offered, based on the experience of personal computer owners.

First and foremost is not the product's cost but its compatibility. Is the memory offered by the small peripheral company totally compatible with your computer? Some chagrined computer owners have purchased seemingly well-designed, quality memory boards from peripheral firms only to find that the new memory required far more electrical power than the computer's power supply was designed to provide.

Other computer enthusiasts have purchased memory boards that used memory chips with too slow an access speed for their computers.

Expensive mismatches like these can often be avoided by carefully comparing the specifications of the various memory boards being considered and those of the computer. When in doubt, ask a dealer or supplier to advise you.

If you're purchasing the RAM from a local dealer, you should consider taking your computer to the store for a live demonstration. Even if the memory board is designed expressly for the computer you own, this reduces the chances of buying a defective board.

NOTE: Many personal computers require the addition of sockets or other hardware before additional memory or other circuits can be added.

Another factor which you should carefully consider when buying more RAM is quality. A neatly assembled double-circuit board loaded with row after row of memory integrated circuits may appear to have been assembled with the greatest care to even the most experienced eye. And it probably was. But was it assembled with prime-quality memory chips?

This question has become very important as the demand for memory chips has increased. Recently, there have been several major scandals involving the sale of faulty memory chips to electronics companies by electronic parts distributors.

In short, if you cannot verify the quality of the parts used in a memory board made by a firm, you're probably better off spending more for a board made by the company that also made your computer. In any event, avoid buying a board that doesn't come with a warranty or guarantee.

Futuristic Memory Developments

In the relatively near future, two new kinds of solid-state memories will become viable, low-cost alternatives to both cassette recorders and floppy disks. They are the charge-coupled device, more commonly known as the CCD, and the magnetic bubble memory. No doubt these names seem quite strange to you now, but you'll be hearing quite a lot about both of these memories if you get involved in personal computing.

In fact, you may already have literally heard from a magnetic bubble memory without realizing it. Bell Telephone Laboratories, the inventor of this new memory, has designed a special bubble memory that stores various spoken words very much like a tape recorder. The memory is used to replace a human telephone operator by informing callers when they have dialed an incorrect number, reached a disconnected number, etc.

Since both CCDs and magnetic bubbles are so important to the future of low-cost personal computing, let's find out a little more about them.

CCD Memories

CCD memories are similar to RAMs since they are silicon integrated circuits. Like RAMs, they lose their stored information when electrical power is removed. And, again like RAMs, they are read-write memories.

The big difference between RAMs and CCDs, however, is the way stored information is organized inside the memory. RAMs, like ROMs, are neatly organized into thousands of addresses where data words are stored. Thanks to random access, information can be retrieved from or stored in any address within a fixed time interval.

Information is stored in a CCD in serial fashion much like data is stored on a cassette tape. This means that it takes more time to store data in and retrieve data from a CCD than a RAM. The data inside the CCD must be reviewed bit by bit to retrieve new data or find an empty address for new data.

By now you're probably wondering why this solid-state analogy of a cassette tape makes a good memory since it's much slower than a RAM. There are two reasons. One is that the CCD doesn't need much electrical power to store information. The other is that each of the thousands of data storage cells in a CCD is much simpler than the cells in a RAM. This greatly increases the amount of data that can be packed onto a memory chip and simplifies manufacture of the chip, too.

Watch for news about CCDs in personal computing periodicals and books if you want to stay abreast of the latest personal computer developments. Already some business computers use them and it's likely some personal computers will soon use them too.

This new CCD memory integrated circuit can store up to 65,536 bits of information.

Magnetic Bubble Memories

One of the most unusual computer memories yet developed, the magnetic bubble memory, may one day replace the floppy disk. That's good news for those who can barely raise the cash for their own computer, much less the $500 or more required to buy a floppy system.

Texas Instruments has already introduced a small business-oriented computer printer that uses a magnetic bubble memory. Several other companies are now hard at work designing bubble memories for the personal computer market.

Since bubble memories are going to become very important in the next several years, you should know something about them. First, while bubble memories are solid-state memories without moving parts, they are completely different from any of the semiconductor memories that we've discussed so far. Their key ingredient is a very thin wafer of magnetic garnet. It's very easy to form small magnetized regions called domains inside such a wafer. The domains can be effortlessly pushed or pulled anywhere within the wafer with the feeble magnetic field produced by a magnetized needle.

These magnetic domains resemble tiny cylinders only a few millionths of an inch in diameter and as long as the garnet wafer is thick. They can actually be seen when viewed through a microscope, and when viewed on end, they resemble tiny bubbles.

It's very easy to create and erase these magnetic bubbles by placing a pattern of tiny metal "T's" and bars on the surface of the garnet. A magnetic field is applied in quick succession to each of several coils of wire mounted near the garnet. This creates a rotating magnetic field and causes the bubbles to move from "T" to bar to "T" and so forth.

As you may have guessed, bubble memories, like CCDs, are serial memories. In some ways, a bubble memory is very similar to a magnetic tape memory system. The difference, of course, is that the data moves through the "tape" (the garnet) and is erased, retrieved, and read out by tiny metal outlines instead of a read-write head.

Bubbles can be whisked through a garnet wafer at more than 10,000,000 per second. This gives a data storage and retrieval time that's slower than some semiconductor integrated circuit memories, but much faster than floppies, and considerably faster than cassettes.

Bell Labs has built a compact bubble memory that holds 270,000 bits. The memory doesn't require power to retain its stored data since, like cassette tapes and floppy disks, magnetic data is non-volatile. All these advantages, plus small size and low operating power, mean bubbles will definitely be an important alternative to floppies in coming years. While bubbles do not offer the convenience of being able to store huge quantities of information in a drawer full of disks, they offer all the other advantages of floppies plus anticipated lower cost at some future time, faster access speed, and smaller size.

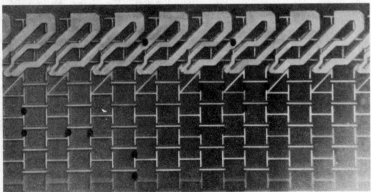

This is a microphotograph of a small section of a bubble memory chip. Note the bubbles (small dark dots).

Extras You Can Add

THE EASIEST way to increase the power of a personal computer is to add more memory. Another way to increase the power and versatility of a computer is to add extra devices that help you get information, in any form you specify, into and out of your computer as quickly and as efficiently as possible. These extras or options are called peripherals.

You already have been briefly introduced to such important peripherals as the teletypewriter, printer, and video monitor or display terminal. Most consumer and appliance computers are supplied with at least a couple of these peripherals, usually a keyboard and video display as well as the electronic circuits required to connect or interface both of these units with the computer. This provides an input-output terminal almost as sophisticated as those used with big computers.

In this chapter, we'll look at the various kinds of printing and video terminals available to the home computer user. We'll also examine some of the special-purpose circuit boards that can be added to many hobby- and some appliance-level machines. These boards contain electronic hardware that can allow a computer to do such remarkable things as talk, respond to spoken commands, synthesize music, and paint full-color electronic pictures.

Even if you're considering an appliance-level machine that is supplied with its own keyboard and video display, you might find some of this information about peripherals of interest. Most peripherals, as you might expect, are expensive. Many cost half as much as, for example, a Radio Shack TRS-80 or Commodore PET. Some cost even more. But some peripherals provide very advanced or specialized features that you might find quite useful.

As you become more involved in personal computing and begin to think about ways of expanding the capabilities of your machine, you may very well want to consider acquiring some of the fascinating add-ons that are available.

Video Display Terminals

A video display terminal (VDT) is the combination of a typewriter-like keyboard for entering information and commands into a computer's memory and a video display to observe the information that's been entered. The display also shows the results of computer operations.

Many types of video terminals are in use. They range from the simple keyboard and display of a pocket calculator to so-called "intelligent" terminals that can function as complete computers on their own.

Nearly all VDTs for personal computers use a cathode ray tube (CRT) similar to the picture tube in a tele-

TV or typewriter? It's a video display terminal, one of the most important parts of a personal computer.

vision set. They're also often called CRT terminals and, sometimes, glass terminals. While VDT terminals do not provide a printed record (hard copy in computer jargon) of your session at the keyboard like the teletypewriters that we'll be discussing later, their silent operation is a pleasant contrast to the loud clickety-clack of printing terminals.

Another big advantage of VDT terminals over teletypewriters is speed. For example, it's often necessary to have a computer display the program that you're writing or working with. If the computer understands BASIC, it will display the complete program when you type the instruction LIST into its keyboard. A teletypewriter terminal, meanwhile, will respond to the instruction LIST by noisily typing each line of the program on a paper roll or tape at a rate of perhaps 10 characters per second. At this rate, a teletypewriter might require several minutes or more to list a relatively long program.

Since the display of a VDT doesn't have any moving parts, it can flash an entire program on its screen much faster than the human eye can follow. This capability speeds up program editing and debugging considerably.

Appliance-grade personal computers like the Commodore PET and the Radio Shack TRS-80 are supplied with either a built-in or attached video display terminal. Hobby computers, however, rarely include a terminal (each section is added separately, as desired), so let's see what's available.

"Dumb" Video Terminals

A "dumb" terminal, as you've probably guessed, provides the minimum equipment required to type pro-

This very basic video display terminal contains a minimum of electronics and sometimes is called a "dumb" terminal.

grams and information into a computer and see the results flashed on a screen. One of the first and still one of the most popular "dumb" terminals is the ADM-3A, made by Lear Siegler, Inc. This terminal is available completely assembled or in kit form.

The ADM-3A is housed in an attractively styled cabinet with a built-in keyboard and CRT. The keyboard has 59 keys and the screen will hold up to 1920 characters. These specifications are fairly typical of other dumb terminals on the market.

"Smart" Video Terminals

The intelligent or "smart" video display terminal is a major improvement over a minimum capability dumb terminal. A typical intelligent terminal like Soroc Technology's IQ 120 has a built-in memory that can store up to a screen-full of characters. The IQ 120 has 73

Video display terminals with many computer-like features are called intelligent or "smart" terminals.

keys and both upper and lower case alphabetic characters. This means that it can be used in such specialized applications as word processing. It also has built-in circuits that enable you to edit what you've typed onto the screen.

Some smart terminals have one or more self-contained microprocessors and can do many things a small computer does. Many of these terminals have a separate calculator-type keyboard adjacent to the main ASCII keyboard for the speedy entry of numbers. This allows the computer to be used like a calculator, often without having to write programs to solve straight-forward problems.

Smart terminals, however, are far too expensive for the average personal computer enthusiast. A quality intelligent terminal easily costs more than $1500, enough money to buy two or three appliance-level computers complete with their own terminals!

The components of this partially disassembled smart terminal show why they are so expensive.

Some hobby computer enthusiasts have purchased intelligent terminals for use with home-built computers. This provides an excellent input-output capability and allows the hobbyist to dedicate more time to the computer's central processing unit (CPU) and memory. The result can be a very powerful computer that more resembles a small business or research machine than a hobby micro.

Graphics Terminals

Terminals designed for producing designs, charts, graphs, layouts, and even computer-generated art on the screen of a cathode ray tube are called graphics terminals. Most small computers and terminals have some graphics capabilities, but terminals designed specifically for graphics can produce pictorial displays with much higher resolution than standard terminals.

This "smart" terminal, made by Digi-Log Systems, includes a pair of built-in floppy disk drives.

Some even produce graphics in full color.

Graphics terminals are expensive, and it's important to compare the ability to make elaborate graphs and pictures on a CRT with the cost of this capability. Unless you've got money to spare or an important application that requires fancy graphics, such as a part-time business, you should consider investing your computer budget in more memory, software, and peripherals like a printer or disk memory system.

Incidentally, for those of you in the market for a graphics terminal, be sure to find out what kind of software, if any, comes with the machine. The elaborate four-color maps, "Star Trek" characters, and graphs that you may have seen in advertising brochures from terminal makers were not created by simply pushing a couple of keys. Fancy graphics require many hours and perhaps even days of program writing. Make sure that you'll be able to use a graphics terminal before you buy one.

The starship image was produced on the screen of an ordinary TV set using a low-cost hobby computer.

With a professional graphics terminal like this that costs nearly $5000, great detail is possible.

Teletypewriter Terminals

Teletypewriter terminals provide a permanent paper record of everything that you type into a computer as well as all of the computer's responses. Computer users call information printed on paper, whether by you or the computer, hard copy. This is why you'll often hear teletypewriter terminals called hard-copy terminals.

In many ways these peripherals look, act, and sound more like an electric typewriter than a computer terminal. You can even use some teletypewriter terminals as a typewriter when the computer is not being used.

For years, the most used hard-copy terminal was Teletype Corporation's ASR-33. This terminal is considered slow by today's standards since it prints only 10 characters per second (10 cps). And, its print quality is not nearly as good as that produced by newer terminals. But many thousands of ASR-33's are still in

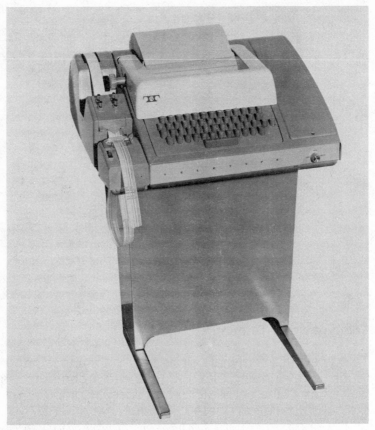

Teletype's ASR-33, around for years, is one of the most reliable and economical teletypewriters available.

use, and there's a booming market for reconditioned units. Some have a special attachment that both reads data from a perforated tape and punches data into new tape for later use.

Teletype Corporation and a host of other companies now sell a wide range of sophisticated teletypewriters that look very much like a standard electric office typewriter. Many of these machines produce very high quality print so that they're ideal for typing individualized letters and reports as well as other word-processing applications.

Teletypewriters are often used in conjunction with a standard video display terminal to save paper, reduce typing noise, and increase efficiency. A form letter, for example, can be silently composed and edited on the quiet keyboard of a VDT terminal. The appropriate number of finished copies can then be printed by the teletypewriter.

The name and address of the first person to whom a form letter is being sent is typed directly into the teletypewriter. The computer then prints the letter automatically and error-free in much less time than you or a secretary would require. The remainder of the letters are prepared in the same manner.

Printers

A printer is a one-way teletypewriter. It prints information under the control of a computer, but it has no provision for entering information into a computer.

What good is a printer that only prints? If you decide to enter the world of personal computing, you'll probably spend most of your time at the keyboard of a video display terminal. As you'll soon learn, however, there will be many times when you'll want to save the information on the VDT screen for future reference.

One way to save the information is to load it onto an unused cassette tape. But this takes time and involves a fair amount of hassle when you need to refer to perhaps only one or two pieces of information that you previously saved, such as a couple of telephone numbers or perhaps a recipe. Often, the best way to save the information is to make a hard copy of it. A teletypewriter can take care of this chore in quick order, but teletypewriters are expensive.

You might consider photographing the information on the screen, but setting up the camera takes time, and you'll need to take a series of pictures if you're interested in saving more information than can be displayed on the screen at one time.

The best way to make a hard copy is to use a printer. Printers are designed for only one job, so most of them are very fast. They can print far more information than that displayed on a screen at any one time since they print on a continuous roll of paper. And they can be quickly ordered into action by pressing a button or with a simple keyboard command.

The combination of a VDT terminal and a printer gives you many of the capabilities of a teletypewriter for significantly less money. But don't build your hopes up. Depending on the model, you can expect to spend from $250 to more than $1500 for a printer designed for use with a hobby- or appliance-level computer.

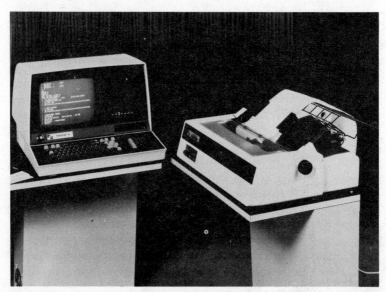

Every computer hobbyist would love to own this smart terminal with self-contained dual floppy drives and hard-copy printer.

Types of Printers

Many different kinds of printers that are suitable for use with personal computers are available to computer enthusiasts. Anyone thinking about adding a printer to a personal computing system should know something about how the various kinds of printers form characters on paper. Printers are classified as either impact or nonimpact.

Most impact printers print characters on paper the same way that a typewriter does. A hammer strikes a movable wheel, ball or cylinder covered with embossed characters and forces a selected character against an inked ribbon. The ribbon then forms a printed outline of the character on the paper.

Lately, a new kind of impact printer has become very popular, particularly in the personal computing field. It's called the matrix or array printer.

There are several kinds of matrix printers. Most have a row of needle-like pins that can be individually fired against a ribbon. Each pin produces a single dot on a paper tape or roll. The pins are installed in a head that moves back and forth across the paper. Characters are formed by selectively firing the pins to produce dot patterns.

Matrix printers are much cheaper and have fewer maintenance problems than impact printers that print entire characters at one time because they have fewer moving parts. But their legibility is not nearly as good.

Some of the latest matrix printers, however, form characters by spacing dots so closely they appear to be continuous lines. This method produces characters almost as clear as impact printers that use embossed characters. These new printers are expensive.

Two kinds of non-impact printers have become very popular with personal computer users owing to their quiet operation, reliability, and relatively low cost, at least low as printers go. These devices produce characters on special paper without the need for a noisy, maintenance-prone hammer mechanism.

One kind of non-impact printer produces blue characters on chemically treated, heat-sensitive paper. Characters are formed by sweeping a print head across the paper in a rapid series of steps. Each time that the print head stops, tiny elements in the head are electrically heated to produce an outline of the desired character.

Paper for such thermal printers is more expensive than ordinary paper, and thermal printing is not very fast. But several calculator companies reported good sales of portable calculators equipped with built-in thermal printers. And, it's likely that low-priced printers for appliance- and hobby-level personal computers will soon become available too.

The second kind of non-impact printer that you should know about uses an electrographic printing process. The key to this printing method is a special electrically sensitive paper that looks and feels more like aluminum foil than ordinary paper. It's actually a three-layer "sandwich" made by coating ordinary paper with black ink and then applying an ultra-thin layer of aluminum over the ink. A black dot, for example, is formed on electrographic paper by passing an electrical current through a whisker-like wire touching the aluminum coating. The electricity removes a small dot of aluminum, exposing a dot of ink.

Characters are formed by sweeping a print head made from a row of whiskers across the surface of a roll of electrosensitive paper. Electrical currents are sent to each whisker at precise intervals to form bars and dots that comprise individual characters.

Since electrographic printers have few moving parts and are very quiet, they're reasonably economical and, therefore, popular with personal computer owners. Their major drawback is the special paper they require. The shiny surface coupled with the low resolution of matrix printing can make characters hard to read. Also, the aluminized surface picks up fingerprints, and it tends to wrinkle easily. And, the special paper is more expensive than ordinary paper.

Impact vs. Non-Impact Printers

Many different factors enter into the selection of a printer for a personal computer. Price is probably the most important consideration for most computer users. But reliability, print quality, noise, paper cost, and availability are also very important.

A printer can be an important addition to an appliance- or hobby-level computer. To help you better evaluate commercially available printers, study the accompanying table comparing the advantages and disadvantages of various kinds of impact and non-impact printers.

Now, we will describe several popular microcomputer printers. They are categorized into three cost ranges: low (below $500), medium ($500-$1000), and high (above $1000). Keep in mind that the printers described are merely representative of what is available. If you're in the market for a printer, be sure to obtain information on other printers from your computer dealer or by writing printer companies that advertise in computer magazines before making a final choice.

Major Characteristics of Impact and Non-Impact Printers.

	LEGIBILITY	SPEED	PAPER COST
IMPACT	good	slow to medium	low
NON-IMPACT	poor to fair	medium to fast	high

	NOISE LEVEL	MOVING PARTS	COST
IMPACT	high	many	low to high
NON-IMPACT	very low to low	few	medium

Low-Cost Printer

At the bottom of the printer line is Southwest Technical Product's PR-40. This impact machine prints up to 40 characters per line on standard 3-7/8 inch wide paper adding machine tape. It can print up to 75 lines per minute. The PR-40 is designed expressly for microcomputer applications. Characters are formed by a matrix of five to seven dots, and are easier to read than characters produced by thermal and electrographic printers.

A kit version of the PR-40 machine can be purchased for about $250. A fully assembled version costs approximately $150 more. The electronic control circuits for the printer are housed in a plain cabinet with a single on-off switch. The printer itself is mounted on top of the cabinet, but doesn't come with a protective

The SWTPC PR-40 is an economical impact printer designed for the hobby computer market.

cover. As printers go, this one is certainly inexpensive, especially if one is able to put together the kit version.

Medium-Priced Printers

Medium-priced ($500 to $1000) printers represent the fastest growing line of computer printers. Both impact and non-impact types are available.

An example of a medium-priced printer is Radio Shack's TRS-80 non-impact screen printer. At the touch of a button, this high-speed electrographic printer will print the entire contents of TRS-80 computer's video display at a rate of 2200 characters per second on a four-inch wide roll of electrosensitive paper. Since the TRS-80 screen holds a maximum of 960 characters, this printer can produce a hard copy of everything on the screen in less than a half second.

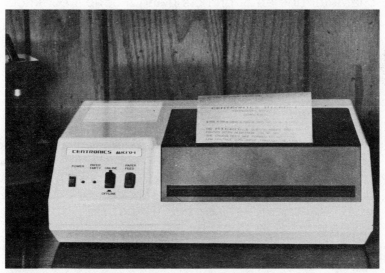

Centronics Data Computer Corp. designed this medium-priced electrographic printer for use with personal computers.

Another popular medium-price printer is the Micro-1 electrographic printer made by Centronics Data Computer Corporation. With a print speed of "only" 240 characters per second, this machine is not as fast as the TRS-80 screen printer. It features a low paper detector, bell, and built-in circuits for interfacing to a microcomputer.

High-Priced Printers

The high-priced end of the personal computer printer market is represented by machines that can also find application in small businesses and educational institutions. But at $1000 or more, these machines easily cost as much or more than an appliance-level microcomputer equipped with 16K of RAM and capable of understanding full BASIC.

Most printers in the low end of the high-priced printer market use some form of impact printing with complete character and array printers being the most common. Their print quality is generally much better than nonimpact, medium-priced printers. And, most of them accept standard letter width or even wider paper. Some can make up to five or more carbon copies of a single print run.

The Centronics 779 is one of the more popular and lower-priced matrix line printers. It prints the standard 64 ASCII characters at up to 110 characters per second. The print density can be adjusted from 10 to 16.5 characters per inch.

The Centronics 703 is an even faster matrix printer. It prints up to 180 characters per second, the equivalent of 120 80-character lines per minute. This rapid print speed is made possible by a printing mechanism that operates as it sweeps back and forth across the paper in both directions.

Few personal computer owners need the capability of a high-priced matrix printer and probably even fewer can afford their $1000-plus price. Some small business

The ALTAIR C700 high-speed impact printer can print up to 60 characters per second.

operators, however, can make efficient use of these printers to rapidly produce hard copy records of inventories, customer lists, billing statements, address labels, and many other paper work chores.

If you are interested in establishing your own lemonade computer company, be sure to consider the business applications and advantages of a fast matrix printer. For example, could you sell custom-printed biorhythms at a shopping center? Are there local firms that might be willing to hire you and your computer to print mailing lists and address labels? With a little thought, you might be able to think of a profitable application for a high-priced matrix printer.

Special-Purpose Circuit Boards

After the ALTAIR 8800, the first commercially successful hobby computer, was introduced in 1975, several small companies sprang up in an attempt to cap-

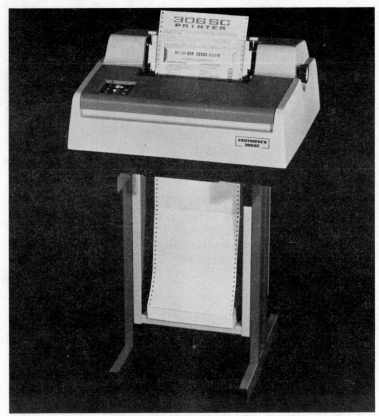

Only computer enthusiasts with hefty budgets can afford a sophisticated printer such as the Centronics 3065C.

italize on its enormous popularity. These companies did not make computers. Instead, they developed various circuit boards that could be installed inside the computer's cabinet alongside the main central processing unit board.

The various electrical connections on the ALTAIR's main CPU circuit board came to be known as the AL-TAIR bus. Because of trademark problems and the arrival of new companies that copied the ALTAIR's con-

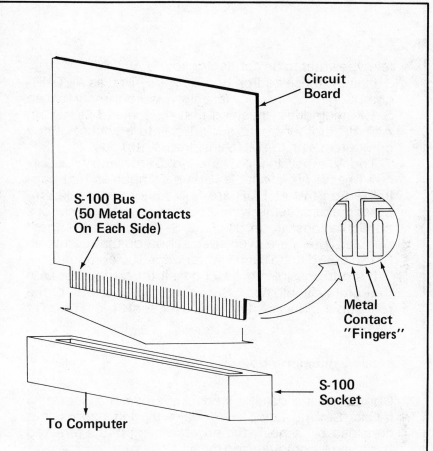

All circuit boards that use the popular S-100 bus can be plugged into S-100 bus hobby computers. This makes it possible to tailor a computer for special-purpose tasks.

nection pattern, it's generally known as the S-100 bus for the electrical connector into which the ALTAIR (and other) CPU board is inserted.

At first, the circuit boards made to fit in the ALTAIR cabinet by companies other than MITS were limited to various kinds of memories. Soon, however, other boards were developed. Cassette interface boards permitted the ALTAIR to accept data from and load data onto a cassette tape. RS232 boards permitted a teletypewriter to be connected to the ALTAIR.

Initially, these add-on boards were billed as ALTAIR-compatible boards. Later, they were simply called S-100 memories, meaning that they would fit into an ALTAIR mother board socket or into a socket of any computer using the MITS-inspired S-100 bus.

Today, a bewildering variety of S-100 and other circuit boards are available. Some companies that capitalized on the ALTAIR are now major personal computer makers themselves. And, though a variety of bus configurations are in use, the S-100 is still the most popular. There are even special boards that permit an S-100 board to be used with a non S-100 computer!

It's not possible to describe all the various boards that are available here. But to whet your appetite, the remainder of this section will cover some more popular ones.

Music Synthesizer Boards

Computers are ideally suited for synthesizing electronic music. Several companies make plug-in boards that considerably simplify the programming that's required to produce computerized music.

One manufacturer is Solid State Music (Cybercom). Its SB1 Music Synthesizer Board can synthesize audio frequencies from 15 to 25,000 Hertz (a Hertz or Hz is a cycle per second). Volume, tempo, tone patterns, attack, and other parameters can be programmed into the computer with the help of MUS-X1, a special music "language" created by Solid State Music.

Unlike simpler computer music synthesizers, MUS-X1 permits music to be produced in "real time," or as the music instructions are being typed into the computer.

If you're interested in exotic electronic music, you'll definitely want to look into the possibilities of boards like the SB1.

Speech Synthesis

There are several intriguing ways to create human speech with computers. None of them, however, are without problems. If you've heard some of these efforts on various television and radio news programs, you know what is meant.

One of the biggest problems in synthesizing purely electronic speech is the enormous amount of memory required. The easiest way to synthesize speech is to simply store a speaker's voice in a computer's memory and "play" it back on demand. This method, which is called digitized speech, requires from 10K to 20K bytes of memory per second of speech! Contrast that with the 4K of memory supplied with most low-cost computers and you can begin to appreciate the problem.

Several companies have developed some very clever ways to synthesize speech with much less memory than that required for digitized speech. One method produces most of the various phonetic sounds of human speech. These are electronically combined, under the direction of a suitable computer program, to produce a reasonable facsimile of human speech. The result is a speech synthesis system that requires only 500 to 900 bytes per second of speech.

If you want to be first on your block with a talking computer, you'll want to look into Computalker Consultants' CT-1 and AI Cybernetic Systems Model 1000 Speech Synthesizer. But be prepared to spend as much as or more than a complete small computer costs to teach your machine to talk.

You'll also need an ample amount of patience because using speech synthesizers can be very difficult. The experience of Leslie Solomon, technical editor of *Popular Electronics* magazine and a home computer pioneer is instructive.

Solomon spent several weeks experimenting with an AI Cybernetic Systems synthesizer and, after spending many hours studying the unit's excellent instructions, succeeded in teaching a hobby computer to speak several recognizable sentences. But considerable patience and hands-on experience was required to reach this point. Solomon concluded by paraphrasing Samuel Johnson:

"Sir, a computer talking is like a dog walking on its hind legs. It is not done well; but you are surprised to find it done at all."

Speech synthesizer boards are so sophisticated—and expensive—that they will be of interest only to serious experimenters with a hefty budget, educational institutions, research institutions, and firms active in the area of speech synthesis. So, unless you're devising a reading machine for the blind or perhaps an electronic message reader for an electronic bank teller, speech synthesis is more of an expensive novelty than a practical application for a home computer.

Speech Recognition Boards

If human brainpower can succeed in finding ways to make computers talk, it follows that someone will try to design a way for a computer to listen. The first speech recognition board for personal computers is SpeechLab, a product of Heuristics, Inc., a speech research company. Here's how it works:

First, the computer must be taught to recognize individual words. This is done by typing the word on the computer's keyboard and then clearly pronouncing the word into a microphone. SpeechLab's circuits quickly analyze the spoken word, convert it into a digital code, and store it in only 64 bytes of memory.

After SpeechLab has been used to teach a computer a vocabulary of words, it's ready to be used. In a popular demonstration by Heuristics at personal computer shows and conventions, a SpeechLab-equipped computer responds like an electronic typewriter by actually printing out words that it has been taught only minutes before, each time a word is spoken into its microphone.

SpeechLab has many potential applications. Handicapped people, for example, could make use of a SpeechLab-equipped computer to control a thermostat, operate a telephone, turn a television on and off, and anything else that can be connected to the computer's output ports. It can even be used to store the various command and statements of BASIC to allow oral computer programming!

While these and other applications are very intriguing, the average computer hobbyist will be better off by investing his computer budget into more practical equipment. But if you're seriously interested in the possibilities of verbal interaction with a computer and have an ample budget for the support equipment that you'll need (a hard copy terminal would be helpful according to one SpeechLab user), see a demonstration. You might find it is the ideal way to control that computer-controlled robot you've been planning to build.

Analog-To-Digital and Digital-To-Analog Converters

Variable or analog information, such as thermostat settings, temperature, light intensity, joystick positions, voltage, and others, must be converted into digital form before it can be entered into and processed by a computer. This function can be accomplished by an analog-to-digital (A/D) converter.

Several personal computer and peripheral companies make A/D converter boards. A typical A/D converter is the Model D+ 7A I/O made by Cromemco, Inc. This S-100-compatible board accepts analog signals from up to seven separate sources and converts each signal into its binary equivalent. The only software instructions required are input and output signals applied to the board by means of the microcomputer bus.

The D+ 7A I/O board can also convert digital information into an analog form. The analog output from the board is a variable voltage that can be used to control such things as the speed of a motor, the brightness of a lamp, the pitch of a tone, and many others.

A/D and D/A boards are available from both computer and peripheral companies. And, while they provide a way to interface a computer with the outside world, it's essential to understand how they are applied, connected, and operated before acquiring one. Sophisticated programming as well as expensive gadgetry may be required to make practical use of an A/D or D/A board.

TV Dazzler

An ordinary color television can be converted into a full-color video display terminal by adding a Cromemco TV Dazzler board to a computer. The Dazzler consists of two S-100 compatible boards that are available in either kit or assembled form. With the help of Cromemco software, the TV Dazzler system can produce colorful kaleidoscopic displays and full-color alphanumeric characters. The circuits require 2K of RAM to store the video patterns that they generate. **NOTE:** A television interface circuit is required.

Other S-100 Boards

Numerous other S-100 boards are available from computer and peripheral makers. Many allow various external devices such as teletypewriters, video display terminals, disk memory systems, and cassette recorders to be connected to a computer. Others allow a computer to control from one to many outside devices, even over a telephone.

As the price of sophisticated hardware continues to drop, it's likely that the number of peripheral boards that can be added to a computer will grow. A good way to keep up with what's available is to read current personal computing magazines.

Where To Find Programs

NO MATTER how powerful a computer is or how many accessories are added to it, without a program a computer is as useful as a television set that is tuned to a blank channel. This chapter describes ways to build up a library of programs should you decide to buy your own computer.

From the beginning, it is important to recall that most consumer-level computers can be operated by almost anyone, including many children. They're not much more complicated to use than TV video games.

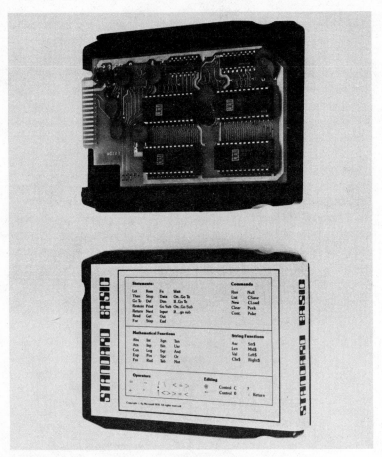

This plug-in cartridge allows a user to program the Sorcerer computer with Standard BASIC.

This chapter, however, applies to appliance- and hobby-level computers. While it is true that a beginner can quickly learn to do relatively simple things with an appliance-level machine, the user eventually will need to employ more sophisticated programs.

Thanks to BASIC, the straightforward language that most appliance- and hobby-level computers understand, most users, with a little experience, will soon be able to create their own programs. But writing programs that work as you want them to takes time. And, writing advanced programs usually requires considerable experience. Fortunately, there are many sources for software that have been developed and debugged by an experienced programmer.

The software from these sources ranges from simple subroutines to highly sophisticated compilers and interpreters. And, its cost ranges from nothing for a few weeks access to a library book full of programs to $10 or more for a prerecorded cassette tape ready to be loaded into a computer.

Like hardware, the effective use of software requires clearly written operating instructions. Often, instructions for a particular program are included as part of the program itself. The program automatically flashes out the instructions on the computer's video display terminal at the appropriate time.

Sophisticated software, however, often requires long and detailed instructions. The cost of writing, printing, and packaging (often in a three-ring binder) software instructions significantly adds to the overall price of commercial software.

Manufacturer-Supplied Software

Unless you've had previous computer experience, it's likely that the first computer programs you'll see beyond those in this book will be supplied with a computer you buy. Most consumer- and appliance-level machines, and some hobby computers, come with an operator's manual that includes a variety of programs to familiarize you with the computer's operation.

The *User's Manual For Level 1* supplied with Radio Shack's TRS-80, for example, includes dozens of sample programs presented in an entertaining self-learning format. Many of the programs are designed to demonstrate each of the BASIC statements that the TRS-80

*Apple II's programming manual guides the beginner
from setting up the computer to writing BASIC programs.*

understands. Some of the programs included are: Fahrenheit-to-Celsius Conversion; Salary Rate Chart; Move the Dot (a simple graphics program); TEST Grading Program; Savings Account Return; 12-Hour Clock; Slowpoke (a reaction time tester); Wheel of Fortune; Dow-Jones Industrial Average Forecaster; Automatic Ticket Number Drawer; and Loan Amortization.

The TRS-80 manual also includes a collection of subroutines that allows the user to employ Level-1 BASIC to solve problems that include mathematical functions such as square root, logarithms, most trigonometric functions, and several others that would otherwise require a more advanced version of BASIC.

Radio Shack and some other personal computer manufacturers also sell software separately. These programs are usually sold in the form of prerecorded cassette tapes. Obviously, prerecorded software can only be used with a computer that is equipped with the appropriate cassette tape interface. As noted earlier, software designed to work with one company's computers may not work with another firm's machines. A slightly different form of BASIC may have been employed, or, the program may have been encoded on the tape using a method that only one company's computers can understand.

Free Software

Considering the price of software that is sold by computer and software companies, it's hard to believe that a substantial amount of free software is available at many libraries. Books about computers, programming, games, mathematics, and many other subjects often include programs in BASIC and other languages.

The best sources of free software are large university libraries. Finding books that include software requires an investment of time and energy, but the time required is far outweighed by the benefits of the free software and any incidental knowledge gained while flipping through books about computers and programming.

Periodicals About Home Computing

A bonanza of software awaits the home computer enthusiast who subscribes to some personal computing magazines. A recent issue of *Personal Computing,* for example, included a complex BASIC program called "Harvest" that allows the computer-equipped amateur horticulturist to scientifically plan virtually every aspect of a home vegetable garden. Also in this issue was a BASIC program for calculating seasonally adjusted price indexes, several clever arithmetic and game programs, and a money-making program that can be used to generate amortization tables for real estate agents, attorneys, lending institutions, and others who borrow and lend money.

If you decide to acquire your own computer or if you

just want to keep abreast of the latest software trends and developments, you should consider subscribing to at least one of the personal computing magazines.

Books About Home Computing

Unfortunately, libraries have been slow to acquire recently published books about home computing. Dozens of new computer books are available and some of them include good selections of software. Ask your computer store manager for recommendations about books on software. He will be able to advise you whether or not you'll be able to use programs listed in a book with a particular computer. Some programs will work with a few minor editing changes, but others may not work at all.

Software Companies

A growing number of companies are being formed to cater to the needs of home computer owners. These range from one-person operations to sophisticated spin-offs from computer companies.

Software companies offer an incredible range of computer programs in languages ranging from microprocessor machine language to higher-level languages like BASIC and FORTRAN. They include text editors, assemblers, interpreters, and compilers as well as numerous kinds of games, graphics, and subroutines.

The price for programs from software companies can be high. Would you believe that one firm charges $15 for a program that allows you to play tic-tac-toe with a hobby computer? The real catch is that the program can only be used with a computer equipped with a $350 circuit board made by the same company. You also need a color TV set!

Nevertheless, bargains in quality software are available. One company, for instance, sells a sophisticated software package that converts a computer into a sophisticated electronic musical instrument for about $25. The price seems high at first, but the compiler has a range of four octaves, can play up to three notes simultaneously, and includes all the standard musical notations (any key, time, signature or clef plus note values from whole notes to 1/64 notes, rests, dotted notes, triplets, etc.)!

Not many home computer operators have either the musical expertise or programming knowledge to produce a music compiler with these advanced capabilities. And, those few who do would have to invest many hours of time to produce a compiler that does everything this one does. In short, while the compiler's $25 price tag may seem high, it's quite reasonable.

Where can one find companies that produce software? Many such firms advertise in personal computing periodicals. If you live in a large metropolitan area, a computer store may be able to refer you to a local software company. Some computer stores also write and sell software.

Custom Software

Computer enthusiasts who become serious about personal computing inevitably reach a point where they want to go beyond the software available from manufacturers, books, and periodicals. The ideal way to generate custom software to fill such a requirement is the do-it-yourself approach. This method costs nothing more than time, and it allows a program to be tailored to the specific needs and peculiarities of the problem at hand. However, the newcomer to personal computing most likely does not have the programming knowledge or experience to generate relatively sophisticated custom software. And, even the experienced computerist may encounter considerable difficulty in attempting to write an advanced compiler or text editor software package.

There are several ways to obtain custom software

services. The most obvious and also the most expensive is to approach a software company. If cost is no problem, this is the way to go.

There are, however, cheaper ways to obtain custom software. You might be able to work out an exchange with a qualified student who cannot yet afford his or her own computer system. The student develops the custom software that you need. In return, you grant a previously agreed upon number of hours at the keyboard of your computer.

The best way to find students who might be able to generate custom software is to attend meetings of a local computer club, but keep in mind that while there are many clever and competent young programmers, it might be difficult to find someone who can solve your particular software problem.

User's Clubs and Exchanges

Still another way to develop a software library is to join a computer user's club or exchange. Several such clubs exist. They're almost always devoted to a specific company's computer or a particular language.

Clubs and exchanges publish newsletters that contain operating hints and tips as well as useful software. Most newsletters are published monthly and an annual subscription or membership usually costs $10 or $15. The membership cost is easily returned several times over by the software and other valuable information you can receive.

Software Licensing Agreements

An important aspect of computer software that you should know about is copyright. Personal computer hardware and software companies spend a great deal of time and money developing software, and it's not too surprising that most try to protect their investments.

A major software controversy arose soon after MITS, Inc., ushered in the era of personal computing with its ALTAIR 8800. MITS went to great lengths to protect the software that it sold to ALTAIR owners, even requiring a purchaser to sign a seven-page licensing agreement. But many customers made copies of software and gave them to friends.

Since software is so easy to copy, some companies have taken a much more relaxed view than MITS. Southwest Technical Products, for example, issued a formal statement on its software policy that takes a more realistic position:

> Unlike some of our competitors, we at Southwest Technical Products Corporation have realized for some time that you can't profitably sell software to hobbyists. Of course, you can always sell a few copies, but before you know it there will be five to ten copies in existence for every one sold. The best alternative as we see it is to absorb the cost of the software within the selling price of the computer itself and only charge that amount necessary to cover the expense of program duplication and handling; and that's just what we are doing. None of the programs available from SWTPC are proprietary. Where available, you may either purchase a tape and instruction manual from us or copy them from a friend. We don't care.

This attitude about software on the part of a hobby computer company makes sense. Of course, companies whose major or perhaps only product is software must protect their investment against unauthorized distribution. In any event, it is important to be aware of any legal responsibilities that you incur when purchasing software, a computer, or other hardware device that is supplied with software. Lawsuits have been brought against persons who have violated software licensing agreements and copyrights.

How To Give Orders To Your Computer

IF YOU ARE like most people who have had no prior computer experience, then you are probably concerned about the prospect of learning to program a personal computer. Of course it's not absolutely necessary for you to learn to program to use a computer. Consumer-level computers instruct you. With the help of prerecorded program tape cassettes or solid-state memory cartridges, you are told exactly what to do. And almost anyone can quickly learn to type many of the thousands of existing programs into the keyboard of an appliance-level microcomputer.

If you are not interested in learning how computers are programmed, you could skip this chapter. But before you do, think about this: Almost everyone already has programming experience!

Consider the pay telephone. Before you can talk with the party you wish to call, you must follow a simple list of instructions that goes something like this:

1. Look up the number of the person you wish to call in a telephone directory.

2. Remove the telephone's receiver from its cradle.

3. Insert the proper amount of money in coins into the appropriate slot or slots.

4. Wait for a tone.

5. Dial the number or push the proper buttons.

This list of instructions seems so simple that you're probably wondering why we've included it. After all, you have probably made thousands of phone calls. The point, of course, is that the instructions in the list comprise a simple program. Though this program is designed for use by a person, it's as much a program as those designed for use by computers.

We use programs to operate many other kinds of devices and machines, ranging from washing machines and stoves to thermostats and jukeboxes. We also use mental programs to perform everyday tasks such as cooking, writing a letter, playing a game, and planning a vacation.

Programming is such an indispensable part of most of our daily activities that it's unfortunate that many

---

NOTE: Up to 64 characters can be displayed across the full width of the screen of a TRS-80 and most other microcomputers. Since this exceeds the column width used in this book, some of the longer lines in the programs that are shown extend to a second line without a line number. If you plan to type any of these programs into a real TRS-80, just consider an unnumbered line as part of the preceding numbered line.

people are intimidated by computer programming. Perhaps the science fiction image of computers as super-intelligent electronic brains is partially responsible for this attitude.

By the time you finish reading this chapter, you'll be well-acquainted with the fundamentals of BASIC, the most common programming language used by personal computers. As you will soon see, BASIC is so easy to learn a beginner can write his own simple programs within a few hours—with or without a computer!

What Is BASIC?

BASIC, an acronym for Beginner's All-Purpose Symbolic Instruction Code, is an advanced computer language. It allows a person to give orders to a computer using ordinary words, phrases, symbols, and numbers. The language was created in 1965 by John Kemeny and Thomas Kurtz, two professors at Dartmouth College, with the help of some of their graduate students.

Just like any other language, BASIC has a vocabulary of words that have very precise meanings. Since BASIC is a two-way language, it allows programs that can simulate conversations between a computer and its operator. And, it produces various messages that tell the operator when the computer is ready to receive new instructions and when an incorrect program instruction or operation has been attempted.

The best way to learn BASIC is to try some actual computer programs written in BASIC. Although having access to a computer is helpful, you don't need one to learn.

After you read this section, you'll probably want to try some of what you've learned with a real computer. For this reason, all the information in this chapter specifically applies to Radio Shack's TRS-80 because this computer is on display in hundreds of Radio Shack stores across the country. This means that you can practice some programs on a demonstrator TRS-80.

Programs in this chapter can be tried on Radio Shack's TRS-80 computer.

You also can get a demonstration of a variety of different kinds of microcomputers at almost any personal computer store. The programs, however, may require minor revisions before they can be used with other computers. This is because some micros use slightly different versions or "dialects" of BASIC.

A Simple Computer Program

Complicated equations and strings of numbers flash through the minds of most people when the word "computer" is mentioned. Since a great deal of this book has been devoted to explaining how the operation of computers is based upon binary numbers, let's work with a simple BASIC program to change the "number-crunching" image computers have.

First, make sure the screen of your imaginary TRS-80 displays:

READY
>—

READY is called a prompt. It tells you that the computer is ready to receive instructions beginning at the location indicated by >—. The dash is called a cursor. It allows you to quickly locate where a character or symbol will appear on the screen after it has been entered from the keyboard.

If the computer's screen does not display READY, find the large white ENTER key on the right side of the keyboard and press it. If READY still fails to appear, the computer may be processing a program (as computers on display in stores are often doing).

Press the key marked BREAK to interrupt the program. Then press ENTER to see the READY prompt. Now you're ready to type the following information into the keyboard (be sure to press the ENTER key after each line of the program):

```
10 PRINT "WELCOME TO THE WORLD OF PER-
   SONAL COMPUTING!"
20 END
```

Did you make an error? No problem, just backstep to the error by pressing the key labeled with an arrow pointing left. Each time you press the key, the cursor will jump one space to the left and erase the character that occupied that position. When you reach the error, type the correction and then type the remainder of the line.

If, however, you notice an error after you've entered a line, you will have to retype the entire line. Use the same line number and the computer will erase the original version containing the error and accept the new line.

Finished? Believe it or not you've just typed a genuine program into a computer. All you have to do to execute or run your program is to type:

RUN

and hit the ENTER key. The computer will then carry out the instruction in your program by showing:

WELCOME TO THE WORLD OF PERSONAL COMPUTING!

This, of course, is an extremely simple program, but it does demonstrate several important rules about BASIC that you should know about.

The first rule is that PRINT is a BASIC language term or statement that orders the computer to display everything, even spaces, bounded by quotation marks following and on the same line as PRINT. You will find PRINT statements to be among the most common of all BASIC operations.

The second rule is that a program should usually be concluded with an END statement. This is to prevent the computer from wandering down into the remnants of some other program that you may have previously entered into the computer.

Another rule you learned is that the ENTER key must be pressed to load each line of a program into the computer's memory. This is very important, but easy to remember since you can think of the ENTER key as the carriage return key on a typewriter. In fact, some micro manufacturers label this key as RETURN or C.R. (Carriage Return).

Notice that the program consists of two lines of text and that each line is preceeded by a number. Without the line numbers, the computer will not consider the information as part of a program.

Why are the lines numbered 10 and 20 instead of 1 and 2? They can, in fact, be numbered 1 and 2. What's more you can use any numbers between 1 and 32767 to number the lines in a TRS-80 program provided that you do not use commas (1,000 instead of 1000). It's customary, however, to number the lines in a BASIC program 10, 20, 30, and so on because this allows you plenty of room to insert extra numbers or steps into the program.

Let's try it. Type the following line into your keyboard:

15 PRINT "COMPUTERS ARE DUMBER THAN YOU THINK."

Now type RUN and press ENTER. The screen will display:

WELCOME TO THE WORLD OF PERSONAL COMPUTING!
COMPUTERS ARE DUMBER THAN YOU THINK.
READY
>—

Notice how the computer automatically inserted the new line into the correct place in the program? We know it did because the monitor's screen flashed the new line of type before displaying the READY prompt, indicating that it had reached the END statement. But we can prove it by using a BASIC command designated LIST. Type:

LIST

into the keyboard, press ENTER, and the screen will display the complete program in numerical order:

>—LIST
10 PRINT "WELCOME TO THE WORLD OF PERSONAL COMPUTING!"

15 PRINT "COMPUTERS ARE DUMBER THAN YOU THINK."
20 END
>—

As you can see, using the statement LIST will cause the computer to display everything put into its memory. Moreover, the computer automatically processes the instructions in a program in numerical order and not the order that they are typed into the keyboard. As you'll see, this convenient feature can save lots of time.

So far, we've learned something about the following BASIC statements, prompts, and concepts: Line Numbers; ENTER; PRINT; Quotation Marks; END; RUN; and LIST.

Now let's liven up the program and learn about several important new features of BASIC by inserting a new line into our program. Type:

15 GOTO 10

Now hit ENTER, type RUN, press ENTER again, and the screen will display 16 repeated renditions of the sentence in line 10 like this:

WELCOME TO THE WORLD OF PERSONAL COM-
PUTING!
WELCOME TO THE WORLD OF PERSONAL COM-
PUTING!
WELCOME TO THE WORLD OF PERSONAL COM-
PUTING!
WELCOME TO THE WORLD OF PERSONAL COM-
PUTING!
WELCOME TO THE WORLD OF PERSONAL COM-
PUTING!
WELCOME TO THE WORLD OF PERSONAL COM-
PUTING!
WELCOME TO THE WORLD OF PERSONAL COM-
PUTING!
WELCOME TO THE WORLD OF PERSONAL COM-
PUTING!
WELCOME TO THE WORLD OF PERSONAL COM-
PUTING!
WELCOME TO THE WORLD OF PERSONAL COM-

PUTING!
WELCOME TO THE WORLD OF PERSONAL COM-
PUTING!
WELCOME TO THE WORLD OF PERSONAL COM-
PUTING!
WELCOME TO THE WORLD OF PERSONAL COM-
PUTING!
WELCOME TO THE WORLD OF PERSONAL COM-
PUTING!
WELCOME TO THE WORLD OF PERSONAL COM-
PUTING!
WELCOME TO THE WORLD OF PERSONAL COM-
PUTING!
WELCOME TO THE WORLD OF PERSONAL COM-
PUTING!

Since this was caused by several major changes in the program, let's cover each of them.

First, we have introduced GOTO, a new BASIC statement. This statement on line number 15 instructs the computer to immediately go to the designated line number, in this case 10, and do whatever is indicated. So GOTO sets up what is called a loop. The computer prints "WELCOME TO THE WORLD OF PERSONAL COMPUTING!," then proceeds to the next instruction, which simply tells it to return to the first instruction!

The result is an endless cycle as the computer continues to flash the specified sentence onto the screen.

The second thing that we have done is to eliminate the step we had earlier added to the program (15 PRINT "COMPUTERS ARE DUMBER THAN YOU THINK.") We did this by simply using the original step's line number for the new step. This caused the computer to automatically erase the old step and remember the new one.,

Still another thing that we did is to make the END statement irrelevant because the computer never gets to it. But we'll leave it in since we are going to modify the program again later.

Incidentally, computer programmers call GOTO an unconditional transfer statement. This definition is necessary to distinguish the GOTO statement from the so-called conditional transfer statement designated IF . . .THEN. . . .

Confused? Just remember that GOTO means the computer has no choice and it must proceed to the indicated line number. A computer programmer would say that GOTO transfers program control to the designated line. IF . . .THEN . . ., as you've probably guessed, gives the computer an option. If a specified condition is met, then program control is transferred to a designated line number. Otherwise, the program continues its normal, step-by-step execution.

Conditional Transfers Using IF . . . THEN . . .

IF . . . THEN . . . makes little sense without an explanation, so let's insert an IF. . .THEN. . . statement in our simple demonstration program to see how it works. The screen of the computer is still displaying those rows of WELCOME TO THE WORLD OF PERSONAL COMPUTING! so we'll have to press the BREAK key to halt the computer. Now let's type the following new steps into the keyboard:

```
05 LET A = 0
12 LET A = 1 + X
13 IF A = 3 THEN 20
```

Remember to press ENTER after you enter each line. Then type RUN and hit ENTER to start the program. The screen will then display:

WELCOME TO THE WORLD OF PERSONAL COMPUTING!
WELCOME TO THE WORLD OF PERSONAL COMPUTING!

WELCOME TO THE WORLD OF PERSONAL
COMPUTING!
READY

>—

As you can see, adding the three new lines
ordered the computer to print the "WELCOME. . ."
message only three times before stopping. Can you
figure out how the new program works?

Don't worry if you're in the dark. We've introduced
a couple of new BASIC concepts, so let's explain
them. First, type LIST and press ENTER to see the
expanded program. The screen of the computer will
display:

```
05 LET A = 0
10 PRINT "WELCOME TO THE WORLD OF PER-
   SONAL COMPUTING!"
12 LET A = 1 + A
13 IF A = 3 THEN 20
15 GOTO 10
20 END
```

Let's assume that we have typed RUN, and are
following the program a step at a time as it's
processed by the computer. Here's an explanation of
what happens:

```
05 LET A = 0
```

This line introduces LET, another new member of
BASIC's vocabulary. It simply establishes a memory
location designated by any letter of the alphabet,
and assigns the number to the right of the equal sign
to the specified location. In this case, memory
location A is assigned the value 0 (or cleared) in
preparation for what takes place in line 12.

10 PRINT "WELCOME TO THE WORLD OF PERSONAL COMPUTING!"

You already know what this line does.

12 LET A = 1 + A

This step seems to contradict itself. If A = 5, then how can 5 = 1 + 5? Actually, this step is not contradictory. Remember that LET assigns a number to a memory location, and in this case the location is designated A. Therefore, LET A = 1 + A simply means that the number stored in A should be changed to the number now in A (which is 0) plus 1.

13 IF A = 3 THEN 20

Here's the IF . . .THEN. . . statement that tells the computer how many times to execute the program. Simply put, IF asks the question: "Is the number stored in memory location A a 3?" If the answer is yes, THEN 13 transfers program execution to line 20 which ends the program. Otherwise, the program continues to line 15, which it does because A only equals 1.

15 GOTO 10

This statement tells the program to return to line 10. The computer then flashes the message in line 10 and advances to line 12 and adds another 1 to memory location A. It then continues to line 13 where it checks to see if the number in A is 3. It's not (A = 2), so the computer arrives at line 15 and the process continues. But the next time through the loop, the number in A reaches 3. Consequently, line 13 transfers program control to line 20.

20 END

The computer comes to a halt and flashes a READY after the three "WELCOME. . ." messages.

Now do you understand how the expanded program works? If so, how would you order the computer to print 10 "WELCOME. . ." messages instead of three?

Well, if you changed line 13 to read IF A = 10 THEN 20, you're absolutely correct. And, you're well on your way to understanding how the IF . . .THEN . . . statement allows programs to establish various kinds of loops.

Incidentally, the number in A (IF A = ?) is called a variable by computer programmers. That's because it can be any number you select.

Loops can be very simple, like the one that we've just analyzed. Or they can be more sophisticated, such as the following one that orders the computer to display a screenful of random numbers:

```
05 CLS
06 LET Z = 0
10 PRINT RND (8); " " ;
15 LET Z = Z + 1
16 IF Z = 240 THEN 30
20 GOTO 10
30 GOTO 30
```

When this program was run on a TRS-80, the following pattern of random numbers was flashed on the screen:

```
1 4 3 1 8 3 2 7 8 8 5 1 3 1 8 8
6 3 8 2 8 6 3 3 3 4 7 6 6 3 8 2
4 5 2 1 5 7 5 4 4 1 3 7 4 3 3 8
4 4 2 6 1 4 7 1 8 5 4 4 2 3 5 7
5 5 2 8 5 6 7 8 1 8 7 1 5 5 6 3
3 8 6 1 7 7 1 4 5 4 5 8 5 2 6 6
1 5 6 3 3 4 7 6 3 5 6 4 2 5 1 2
8 7 2 7 4 3 2 5 7 2 7 1 1 4 3 4
```

```
7 4 3 1 2 5 8 6 3 1 5 6 6 6 5 8
3 1 1 6 4 4 4 6 6 5 8 4 2 4 6 1
7 2 7 8 5 5 1 4 6 2 8 4 3 3 3 6
3 7 1 5 8 5 7 8 8 6 3 6 1 7 7 7
6 6 6 4 6 7 3 8 4 1 4 5 5 1 3 6
6 6 6 1 5 2 3 6 4 5 6 5 1 8 7 7
5 1 5 5 1 7 8 4 4 5 7 7 5 3 7 2
>—
```

This program introduces a couple of new BASIC terms so let's see how it works.

05 CLS

This means "clear screen." It removes everything so that the full screen is available for printing. In this case, CLS is not absolutely necessary because the extraneous material will be automatically removed from the screen as the lines of numbers are flashed on the screen. Its use here simply makes for a neater presentation of the random numbers.

06 LET Z = 0

This assigns a value of 0 to memory location Z.

10 PRINT RND (8) ; " " ;

RND is short for "random number." RND (8) converts the computer into an electronic "die" that automatically generates random numbers between 1 and 8, just as if a die was thrown on a table in the game of craps. Any number can be inserted inside the parentheses. For example, RND (100) would generate random numbers between 1 and 100.
PRINT tells the computer to flash the selected random number on the screen. The remainder of the line (; " " ;) tells the computer to "print" a single blank space after the selected random number to

separate the numbers.

The semicolons instruct the computer to fill a line with random numbers before advancing to the next line. Without ; " " ;, the screen would display a maximum of 16 random numbers in a single column along the left side of the screen.

```
15 Z = Z + 1
16 IF Z = 240 THEN 30
20 GOTO 10
```

These lines establish a loop that orders the computer to generate 240 random numbers. That's equivalent to 15 lines containing 16 numbers each. When all 240 numbers are on the screen, the IF . . .THEN. . .statement orders the program to move to line 30.

```
30 GOTO 30
```

This line is a "do-nothing" step. It tells the computer to establish a loop that seemingly does absolutely nothing! Actually, this step serves a useful purpose. If line 30 was an END statement, the screen would flash a READY prompt and erase two full lines of random numbers. GOTO 30 flashes only the cursor and erases none of the random numbers.

There's one catch about using a step like 30 GOTO 30. To enter new information, the BREAK key must be pressed because once the screen is full of random numbers the program will continue endlessly at line 30.

Using FOR. . .NEXT To Establish Loops

How would you like to reduce the program that fills the computer screen from seven to only five steps? A new BASIC expression called FOR. . .NEXT permits a programmer to do just that. Here's what the new version of the program looks like alongside the original one:

<table>
<tr><td>NEW PROGRAM (FOR. . .NEXT)</td><td>OLD PROGRAM (IF. . .THEN. . .) .</td></tr>
<tr><td>05 CLS</td><td>05 CLS</td></tr>
<tr><td>07 FOR Z = 1 TO 240</td><td>06 LET Z = 0</td></tr>
<tr><td>10 PRINT RND (8);'''';</td><td>10 PRINT RND (8); '' '' ;</td></tr>
<tr><td>15 NEXT Z</td><td>15 LET Z = Z + 1</td></tr>
<tr><td>30 GOTO 30</td><td>16 IF Z = 240 THEN 30</td></tr>
<tr><td></td><td>20 GOTO 10</td></tr>
<tr><td></td><td>30 GOTO 30</td></tr>
</table>

Both programs accomplish exactly the same function of filling the screen with 240 random numbers. Compare the two programs, however, and you'll find that the new program omits all four lines (lines 6, 15, 16, and 20) originally used to set up the loop that tells the computer to generate and print the random numbers.

The new program replaces the four lines associated with the IF . . . THEN . . . expression of the original program with only two FOR . . . NEXT lines. Here's how the new program works:

05 CLS

07 FOR Z = 1 TO 240

Line 5 clears the screen, and line 7 stores a 1 in a memory location designated Z.

10 PRINT RND (8); '' '' ;
15 NEXT Z
30 GOTO 30

Line 10 selects and prints a random number. Line 15 then orders a 1 to be added to the number in memory location Z. The cycle then continues over and over again. After 240 random numbers have been displayed on the screen, line 15 is no longer valid so the computer advances to the next line, which in this case is 30.

As you can see, FOR. . .NEXT can be much more efficient than IF. . . THEN. . .under certain circumstances. IF. . .THEN. . .is still very useful, particularly since the variable can be a number in any designated memory location instead of a fixed number. For example, IF A = B THEN 100. This allows for some very clever programming tricks.

A very useful application for FOR. . .NEXT is as a so-called timer. The random number programs that we have been tinkering with are very fast. For example, the second one fills the screen of a TRS-80 computer with 240 numbers in about six seconds! Suppose that you want to slow down the computer a bit, in fact quite a bit, so that it flashes a new random number each second or so. A FOR. . .NEXT timer is the way to do this. Here's what the timer looks like:

```
12 FOR B = 1 TO 475
13 NEXT B
```

As you can see by the line numbers, the timer fits neatly between lines 10 and 15 of the short version of our random number program. How does it work? Simple! When the computer reaches line 12, it dumps a 1 in a memory location called B. Line 13 then instructs the computer to return to line 12 and place a 2 in B. The process continues, all the while using up time, until the number in B is 475. The program then continues to the next random number selection. Result? The random numbers appear on the screen at about one second intervals thanks to the delay caused by the FOR. . .NEXT timer.

Another use for FOR. . .NEXT is in various kinds of

programs involving arithmetic. We'll look at several such applications later, but first, let's examine another very important nonarithmetic role of the computer.

Conversational Programming

Few features of computers are as impressive as their ability to carry on a "conversation." Naturally, the computer's side of the conversation must be programmed, but the result can greatly simplify the use of a computer by a beginner because its screen can display instructions about what to do.

A key BASIC statement for implementing conversational programs is INPUT. This statement has the same effect as PRINT, and it allows the program to accept information from the keyboard. Here's a simple example of a program that uses INPUT:

```
10  INPUT "HOW MUCH DO YOU WEIGH IN
       POUNDS"; P
20 PRINT "YOUR METRIC WEIGHT IS"; P * .4534
       "KILOGRAMS."
30 END
```

Line 10 flashes the question HOW MUCH DO YOU WEIGH IN POUNDS? on the computer's screen. A question mark is not needed in the program since IN-PUT automatically inserts it. The presence of the P after the semicolon tells the computer to stop and await an entry from the keyboard. After the keyboard entry is made, the weight in pounds is loaded into a memory location designated P. The computer then proceeds to line 20.

Line 20 tells the computer to display YOUR METRIC WEIGHT IS ____ KILOGRAMS. Everything inside quotation marks is automatically printed and the semicolons tell the computer to print everything on the same line. P * .4534 introduces a couple of new ideas, however, so let's study them.

P is the label assigned to the memory location that stores your weight in pounds. The number .4534 is the conversion factor by which a weight expressed in pounds must be multiplied to obtain its metric equivalent in kilograms. And * is the BASIC symbol for multiplication. The usual multiplication sign, X, is not used because it can be confused with a memory location by the computer or the programmer.

Now that you have seen how the program works, let's run it on the computer. Assume the program is entered and that you've typed and entered RUN. The screen will display:

HOW MUCH DO YOU WEIGH IN POUNDS?—

The computer is ready to receive your weight, so type in 158 (or whatever your weight happens to be). The screen will now display:

HOW MUCH DO YOU WEIGH IN POUNDS? 158
YOUR METRIC WEIGHT IS 71.6372 KILOGRAMS.
READY
>—

Impressed? While the effect may not be very effective with an imaginary computer, it's very impressive when tried on an actual computer in front of onlookers.

Here's another example of a program that uses INPUT to ask a question and PRINT to deliver a response:

```
10 INPUT "HOW MUCH MONEY DID YOU EARN
   LAST YEAR"; M
20 PRINT "UNLESS YOU RECEIVE A SUBSTAN-
   TIAL RAISE, YOU WILL"
30 PRINT "HAVE TO WORK"; 1000000000/M;
   "YEARS TO EARN A"
40 PRINT "BILLION DOLLARS!"
50 END
```

You should have no trouble understanding how this program works since we've introduced only two new BASIC rules. The first is that a long line of text can be split into a series of PRINT statements. The second is that BASIC uses the symbol / to indicate division.

Assuming that your income last year was $15,000, here is what the screen will display after the program has been entered and run:

HOW MUCH MONEY DID YOU EARN LAST YEAR? 15000
UNLESS YOU RECEIVE A SUBSTANTIAL RAISE, YOU WILL
HAVE TO WORK 66666.7 YEARS TO EARN A BILLION DOLLARS!
READY
>—

Some conversational programs are amazingly complex and can carry on almost human-like conversations. Many personal computer enthusiasts enjoy developing such programs to demonstrate to other computer owners as well as friends and family members.

An important BASIC operation that makes possible more advanced conversational programs is known as the string function. A string is simply a group of keyboard characters or symbols. It can be a sentence such as HOW ARE YOU?, a name, an address, a telephone number or a list of characters such as (8 P?4S;+G.

A string is designated by the $ sign and assigned to a memory location indicated by a letter of the alphabet. The TRS-80 computer with LEVEL-I BASIC, for example, can accept only two strings, A$ and B$. Each string is limited to a maximum of 16 characters.

More advanced versions of BASIC have much more powerful string functions. For example, TRS-80 LEVEL-II BASIC can assign a string function to any character of the alphabet. Furthermore, each string can contain up to 255 characters.

The string function is very important in word processing, a computer application that is becoming increasingly popular.

Word Processing

Word processing terminals permit newspaper and magazine writers to type their material directly into a computer. The terminal allows mistakes to be corrected and revisions to be made much faster than with traditional pencil and paper methods. And, the final copy can be stored on magnetic tape that can be read out by automatic typesetting equipment.

Another very common use for word processing is generating "personalized" form letters. Here's a program for a form letter that a congressman's secretary can use to speed up answers to mail from constituents:

```
05 CLS
10 INPUT "WHAT IS THE VOTER'S TITLE AND
   LAST NAME"; A$
20 INPUT "WHAT IS THE VOTER'S FIRST NAME
   ONLY"; B$
30 PRINT
40 PRINT
50 PRINT "DEAR"; A$; ":"
60 PRINT
70 PRINT "THANK YOU FOR YOUR LETTER, "; B$;
   "."
80 PRINT "I'M ALWAYS GLAD TO HEAR FROM
   VOTERS LIKE YOU."
90 PRINT "BE ASSURED I'LL TAKE YOUR VIEWS
   INTO ACCOUNT."
100 PRINT
110 PRINT                          "REGARDS,"
120 PRINT
130 PRINT                    "W. E. TAXMORE"
140 PRINT
```

```
150 PRINT
160 PRINT "IF YOU WANT TO PREPARE AN-
     OTHER LETTER, TYPE RUN."
```

As you can see, this program is little more than a series of PRINT statements preceeded by a couple of INPUT statements that assign the voter's full name and first name to two strings, A$ and B$.

Notice the space after "DEAR " in line 50? A space is needed here (and after LETTER in line 70) because TRS-80 strings are placed directly adjacent to any text that is to be printed. The space inside the quotation marks makes certain that the letter will read "DEAR VOTER" and not "DEARVOTER."

Incidentally, look at the PRINT statements in lines 30, 40, 60, 100, 120, 140, and 150. These lines print nothing on the computer's screen. They simply skip lines to provide spaces in the final text.

Here's how the program is used to respond to MR. FED-UP TAXPAYER, a hypothetical constituent. First, the program asks for the constituent's name:

WHAT IS THE VOTER'S TITLE AND LAST NAME?
MR. TAXPAYER
WHAT IS THE VOTER'S FIRST NAME ONLY? FED-
UP

After the first name is entered, the screen displays the text of the personalized letter:

DEAR MR. TAXPAYER:

THANK YOU FOR YOUR LETTER, FED-UP.
I'M ALWAYS GLAD TO HEAR FROM VOTERS LIKE YOU.
BE ASSURED I'LL TAKE YOUR VIEWS INTO AC-COUNT.

REGARDS,
W.E. TAXMORE

IF YOU WANT TO PREPARE ANOTHER LETTER,
TYPE RUN.
READY
>—

Of course a printer is necessary to make full use of a computer's word-processing capabilities, but think of all the applications that one can find for a word-processing micro. Some of the many possibilities include personalized correspondence, mailing lists, and record keeping.

Using a Micro As a Calculator

Now that we've seen how computers, particularly personal computers, can be used for many applications having little or nothing to do with arithmetic, let's look at some of the more traditional roles for which computers are used.

A useful feature of the BASIC used by many personal computer companies is the so-called "calculator mode." Assume that you're seated before the keyboard of a TRS-80. Type:

PRINT 4 + 5

and press ENTER. The screen instantly responds with:

9

The computer can also subtract (-), multiply (*), and divide(/) . For example:

```
PRINT 3 * 4 * 5 * 6
360
```

and:

```
PRINT 123456/654321
.188678
```

Of course you can easily perform all these operations with a low-cost, four-function pocket calculator. The computer only begins to outperform a calculator when it is used in its programming mode.

All of the BASIC operations that we have already learned about as well as several others can be applied to programs involving numbers. Two new BASIC functions you should know about that are often used in arithmetic applications are designated READ and DATA. Let's see how they work.

Using READ and DATA in Arithmetic Programs

READ commands the computer to literally read the number in one or more designated memory locations. The numbers in the locations are supplied by DATA. Confused? Then here's a simple program that shows how READ and DATA are used:

```
10 READ A, B
20 LET Q = A + B
30 LET S = A - B
40 PRINT Q/S
50 DATA 14, 63
60 END
```

After this program is entered and run, the screen of the computer will immediately display:

```
-1.57143
```

Do you understand how the program arrived at this value? Let's review the program a step at a time to make sure:

10 READ A, B

This READ statement tells the program to read the data stored in memory locations A and B in preparation for the next two steps.

20 LET Q = A + B

This step establishes a memory location identified as Q and loads it with the sum of the numbers in locations A and B.

30 LET S = A - B

Another memory location, S, is established and loaded with the difference of the numbers in A and B.

40 PRINT Q / S

This operation wraps up the program by dividing the number in Q by the number in S and flashing the result on the screen.

50 DATA 14, 63

Here is the data that's loaded into memory locations A and B described in line 10. The first number (14) is loaded into the first memory location (A), and the second number (63) is loaded into the second memory location (B).

How does the computer get to the data in time to use it when it's given at the end of the program? Simple. The computer automatically reads any DATA statements that are in the program no matter where they are located. It is customary, however, to place DATA statements at the beginning or end of a program, but they can be placed anywhere.

READ and DATA are very useful, particularly since many different pieces of DATA can be placed in a program. But there's another way to supply numbers to a computer.

Using INPUT in Arithmetic Problems

In the discussion about conversational programs earlier in this chapter, we learned how INPUT can be used by the computer to ask the operator the value of some variable, such as age or weight. INPUT can also be used to ask a series of questions, as in this revised version of the program that we looked at earlier:

```
10 INPUT "WHAT IS THE VALUE OF A" ; A
20 INPUT "WHAT IS THE VALUE OF B" ; B
30 LET Q = A + B
40 LET S = A + B
50 PRINT " A + B DIVIDED BY A - B IS " ; Q / S
60 GOTO 10
70 END
```

As you can see, this program eliminates the READ and DATA statements, and simply asks for the information that it needs. After the computer displays the result, line 60 recycles the program to the first line and the computer asks the first question again.

Using FOR...NEXT...in Number Applications

So far, we have not asked the computer to solve problems any more complicated than those a pocket calculator can easily solve. The FOR...NEXT... operation, however, allows us to write programs that order the computer to rapidly solve a series of problems and present the results in neatly tabulated rows on its screen.

For instance, here's a simple program that squares

the numbers between 1 and 10 and displays the results:

```
10 FOR N = 1 TO 10
20 PRINT "THE SQUARE OF"; N; "IS"; N * N
30 NEXT N
40 END
```

Type RUN, press ENTER, and the screen will display:

```
THE SQUARE OF 1 IS 1
THE SQUARE OF 2 IS 4
THE SQUARE OF 3 IS 9
THE SQUARE OF 4 IS 16
THE SQUARE OF 5 IS 25
THE SQUARE OF 6 IS 36
THE SQUARE OF 7 IS 49
THE SQUARE OF 8 IS 64
THE SQUARE OF 9 IS 81
THE SQUARE OF 10 IS 100
```

Try that with a calculator! Of course a calculator can easily square this sequence of numbers, but it cannot present the results in a neatly tabulated form complete with explanations.

Let's make the program fancier by having the computer display the numbers 1 through 10, their squares, their cubes, and their reciprocals (one divided by the number). Here's the new program:

```
10 PRINT "NUMBER", "SQUARE", "CUBE", "RE-
   CIPROCAL"
20 FOR N = 1 TO 10
30 PRINT N, N * N, N * N * N, 1/N
40 NEXT N
50 END
```

The commas in line 10 establish four columns complete with titles. Line 30 supplies the information for the four columns. Run this program and the screen will display:

NUMBER	SQUARE	CUBE	RECIPROCAL
1	1	1	1
2	4	8	.5
3	9	27	.333333
4	16	64	.25
5	25	125	.2
6	36	216	.166667
7	49	343	.142857
8	64	512	.125
9	81	729	.111111
10	100	1000	.1

This should impress the most ardent calculator user! And, it's only a trivial example of what can be done with the help of FOR...NEXT... and PRINT.

Let's look at another example of how FOR ...NEXT... can be used. The following program generates the complete multiplication table for the digits 1 through 10 in less than three seconds:

```
05 CLS
10 PRINT "THE MULTIPLICATION TABLE"
20 PRINT
30 FOR X = 1 TO 10
40 PRINT X; " ";
50 NEXT X
60 PRINT
70 FOR Y = 2 TO 10
80 FOR Q = 1 TO 10
90 PRINT Y * Q; " ";
100 NEXT Q
110 PRINT
120 NEXT Y
130 GOTO 130
```

If programming appeals to you, why not spend a few minutes figuring out how this program works using what you have learned so far. Remember, though, you do not have to know how a program works to use it.

Computers As Teachers

As you have just seen, computers can solve various kinds of arithmetic problems. They can even be programmed to teach people how to solve arithmetic problems.

Here's a very simple BASIC program that converts a TRS-80 into an electronic multiplication teacher:

```
05 CLS
10 LET R = RND (10)
20 LET Q = RND (10)
30 PRINT "WHAT IS"; R; "TIMES"; Q;
40 INPUT V
50 LET S = R * Q
60 IF S = V THEN 90
70 PRINT "SORRY, PLEASE TRY AGAIN..."
80 GOTO 30
90 PRINT "CONGRATULATIONS! THAT'S COR-
      RECT."
100 PRINT "TYPE RUN IF YOU WANT TO TRY AN-
      OTHER PROBLEM."
```

Here's a sample run of this interesting program:

```
WHAT IS 7 TIMES 3? 22
SORRY, PLEASE TRY AGAIN...
WHAT IS 7 TIMES 3? 21
CONGRATULATIONS! THAT'S CORRECT.
TYPE RUN IF YOU WANT TO TRY ANOTHER
PROBLEM.
READY
>—
```

Can you explain how the program works? Since you've already been introduced to all the BASIC statements used in the program, you should be able to figure it out. Again, it's not necessary to understand how the program works to use it. Even professional computer programmers often use programs developed by others without taking the time to analyze them line by line.

A program like this can make learning the multiplication table fun for elementary school students. Teaching programs can be designed to present many different kinds of arithmetic problems. They can even be designed to teach facts (history, grammar, dates, etc.) and foreign languages!

Going Further

We have introduced many of the statements that comprise BASIC. There are many other BASIC statements and operations, and you will want to learn how they are used if you're interested in learning more about programming.

One area that you will want to cover is BASIC shortcuts. These are the tricks and abbreviations that one can use to condense programs. Another is the use of subroutines, or programs within a program that are referred to over and over as the main program is being run.

A number of excellent books about BASIC are available. If you want to learn more about this computer language, you should obtain one or more of them. Here are some that you should consider:

BASIC and the Personal Computer by Thomas A. Dwyer and Margot Critchfield (Addison-Wesley Publishing Company, 1978).

BASIC: A Programmed Text by Seymour Hirsch (John Wiley & Sons, Inc., 1975).

Basic BASIC by James S. Coan (Hayden Book Company, Inc.).

101 Basic Computer Games by David H. Ahl (Creative Computing).

Some Common BASIC Programs by Adam Osborne (Adam Osborne and Associates, Inc.).

User's Manual for LEVEL I by David A. Lien (Radio Shack, 1978).

What To Do After You Hit Return (People's Computer Company).

These and other books about BASIC are available at many computer stores. Before purchasing a programming book, be sure to consult one of the store's salespersons. Since several dialects or versions of BASIC are in use, you will want books that most closely describe the BASIC used by the computer you might be planning to buy.

Remember that you can learn many fundamentals of BASIC without having access to a personal computer. Remember too, that many computer stores will be happy to let you try out some of the things that you've learned here at the keyboard of a real micro. So, consider investing the time to visit a store or, perhaps, a university or personal computer club where you can get your hands on a computer for an hour or so. Even a brief session at the keyboard should soon convince you that BASIC is a very forgiving and very easy-to-learn computer language.

Guide To Buying a Computer

THE MAIN objective of this book is to provide enough information to permit the average consumer to make intelligent decisions when considering the purchase of a personal computer. At this point, it would be convenient to include a detailed listing of the scores of personal computers that are now available and compare their various capabilities, specifications, advantages, and disadvantages.

The personal computer market, however, is far too complex for any such listing to be complete. The market is also very dynamic, with new companies arriving on the scene virtually every month. Furthermore, since the number of personal computer companies shows signs of exceeding the available market, an industry "shake-out" appears inevitable.

To avoid the risks associated with a detailed listing of personal computers, representative micros from each of three categories—consumer, appliance, and hobby—have been selected. A series of questionnaire-style checklists that will help you evaluate the various features and advantages and disadvantages of competing computers is included.

NOTE: Under no circumstances should you limit your selection to the computers included. Many other computers are currently available and new ones are introduced on a regular basis by both established and new computer companies.

Instead, consider the machines described as representative of what is available. You'll pick up some valuable tips about what to look for in a machine as well as what to overlook when making a decision about purchasing a personal computer.

How To Choose a Computer

Earlier, the subject of selecting a personal computer was discussed. This is an appropriate time to review some of the suggestions and tips, and put them in a checklist form that will help you evaluate and compare various computers. First, it is important to give careful consideration to why you want to buy your own computer.

Can you afford your own computer? Will the system that you would like to purchase require the addition of various peripherals before you can make full use of it? How much does software for the computer cost?

If your primary application is mathematical, will a pocket calculator meet your requirements? Some calculators are very sophisticated and easily surpass a personal computer with limited 4K BASIC.

Are you mainly interested in the recreational aspects of personal computers? Some new TV video games will keep you entertained for hours with their repertoire of full-color games.

Do you simply want to learn how to program a computer? Many community colleges offer inexpensive courses in computer programming.

Do you want to use a personal computer as an electronic file cabinet? Old-fashioned filing methods are not as up to date as a lightning-fast computerized filing system.

If you're still intrigued with the prospect of owning and using your own personal computer after considering these questions, you're ready to begin comparing the capabilities and features of available computers.

Earlier, personal computers were divided into three broad categories: consumer, appliance, and hobby. You might want to refer back to that section for a quick review of each category if you've skipped ahead or forgotten the characteristics that distinguish each.

Despite the vast differences in appearance and capability of the micros in each category, all personal computers share many common operating features and considerations. Some of these concern hardware, or the physical circuits that constitute a computer. Others deal with software, the programs that tell the hardware what to do and how to do it. Still others concern general considerations such as warranties, service, and manufacturer's reliability.

The following questionnaire-style checklists have been compiled to help you evaluate the hardware, software, and more general considerations of various kinds of microcomputers. Few, if any, personal computers will achieve a perfect response score to all questions in each category.

Hardware Considerations

1. Does the computer include a self-contained video monitor?

2. If the machine is intended to be connected to a standard television set, are the appropriate interface circuits and cables provided and, if so, are they approved by the Federal Communications Commission?

3. Does the computer have a graphics capability?

4. Can the computer save information and programs on cassette tapes with the help of a low-cost cassette recorder? If so, is the appropriate circuitry, the so-called cassette interface, included with the computer, or must it be purchased separately?

5. Are a wide range of peripherals available that will permit the computer to be upgraded after it's been purchased?

6. Is the computer designed with the user in mind? For example, if a keyboard is present, does it use standard typewriter format or an odd layout? Is the video display terminal easy to view? If cables are required to interconnect parts of the computer, are they both easy to connect and conceal?

7. Is the price of the computer and its peripherals competitive?

8. Is the computer UL-approved?

Software Considerations

1. Can software from sources other than the computer's manufacturer be used with the computer?

2. Is software readily available?

3. If software is not readily available, how expensive is the software that is available?

4. Is the computer supplied with a user's manual that describes all of the machine's operating features?

5. Does the user's manual include a detailed explanation of the computer's programming language, including the idiosyncrasies, if any, that are so common to personal computers?

Other Considerations

1. Do the hardware and software capabilities and features of the computer fulfill all or most of your requirements?

2. Will the computer be as current and usable in future years as it appears to be now?

3. Does the manufacturer provide a warranty?

4. Is service readily available?

5. What is the manufacturer's reputation?

6. Do you know anyone who has purchased a similar or identical computer made by the manufacturer? If so, have you asked this person for a personal evaluation of the product? Will you be able to exchange software with others who own the same computer?

There are other purchase considerations that you should know about but they apply to micros in only one or two categories. The most important of these will be covered later prior to a discussion about representative consumer, appliance, and hobby computers. Meanwhile, let's devote some time to the microprocessors that make personal computers possible. Several different microprocessors are used in various personal computers and you should know something about their capabilities.

About Microprocessors

The electronic brain of every personal computer is the microprocessor. It is an integrated circuit that contains all of the electronics necessary to form the central processing unit of a digital computer. Add some memory to a microprocessor and you get a microcomputer.

All microprocessors incorporate at least some memory right on the tiny semiconductor chip that contains the microprocessor circuits. Some include a few thousand bits of memory—or even more—and qualify as true single-chip microcomputers.

Some microprocessor chips can perform certain operations better than other chips, so various microprocessors are evaluated according to the following features and capabilities:

1. SPEED: The faster a microprocessor processes

instructions fed into it, the more rapidly it executes a program.

2. MEMORY: Most microprocessors available today and used in the current range of personal computers can access up to 65,536 (65K) 8-bit bytes of RAM memory. Since a typical personal computer has between 4K and 16K bytes of RAM memory, few microprocessors fall behind in the memory department. In coming years, the price of additional memory is expected to drop considerably. When this occurs, the amount of memory that a microprocessor can access will become an important consideration.

3. NUMBER OF BITS: Most of today's personal computers use microprocessors that process information in 8-bit bytes. Some newer microprocessors, however, process information in 16-bit words. This means that more instructions can be processed in a given time interval, which means faster program execution. It also means that considerably more memory can be accessed. Personal computers of the future may use these new 16-bit microprocessors.

4. INSTRUCTION SET: The instruction set of a microprocessor is a listing of all the various operations that the microprocessor can perform. These include such seemingly meaningless operations as "load the accumulator," "shift left," "rotate right," "push," and many others.

While these operations seem totally indecipherable to the novice, they enable a microprocessor to retrieve a binary number from memory, take it apart or combine it with another binary number and insert it back into memory. Complex combinations of these instructions, which must be translated into binary numbers before they can be accepted by a microprocessor, form BASIC and other higher-level computer languages.

The instruction set of a microprocessor may include from 50 to more than 150 different instructions. More instructions permit more efficient programs that operate faster than programs that use more limited instruction sets.

When you're studying the personal computer market, you'll quickly encounter various microprocessor names and designations such as 8080, 6800, 6502, Z80, F8, CDP1802, and others. It's difficult to specify which of these microprocessors is "better" than the others when used in a particular microcomputer, because a cleverly designed computer made with a relatively primitive microprocessor can process programs faster and more efficiently than a poorly designed computer that uses the most sophisticated microprocessor available. As a general rule, however, microprocessors with long instruction sets and fast operating speed are superior to slower microprocessors with more limited instruction sets. Thus, even though there are more similarities than differences among microprocessors, the Z80 and 8085 are generally considered superior to most other 8-bit microprocessors currently available.

Intel's 8086 central processing unit is designed to deliver 10 times the performance of Intel's 8080 CPU.

Consumer Computers

Consumer computers are the simplest and least sophisticated of personal computers. They are designed for mass-market appeal and in some ways more closely resemble super video games than personal computers. The most appealing aspect of consumer computers—the emphasis on prerecorded program tapes or modules rather than do-it-yourself programming—is also their most important drawback.

Many potential computer users haven't the time or interest necessary to learn even the most elementary aspects of computer programming. For them, a consumer computer can be an ideal selection. But even an untrained user can type readily available free or low-cost programs into the keyboard of an appliance-level micro. These machines will also accept prerecorded program cassettes. So be sure to at least have a look at the appliance computer field before selecting a consumer machine.

The checklists of hardware, software, and general considerations given earlier apply to consumer computers and more advanced appliance- and hobby-level micros, so be sure to refer to them if you're considering the purchase of a consumer-level machine.

Here are some additional considerations that apply only to consumer computers:

1. Is the machine user-programmable?

2. If the computer can be programmed by the user, what language is used and how much RAM memory is allocated for storing programs (4K bytes is a reasonable minimum)?

3. Is there more than one source for software?

4. Is the cost of manufacturer-supplied software excessive?

5. Does the computer function more like an advanced TV video game than a computer?

After you have given careful consideration to these points as well as those listed earlier, you'll be better

The VideoBrain, made by the VideoBrain Computer Co.

equipped to make a purchasing decision. To give you some ideas about what to expect in a typical consumer computer, let's consider the VideoBrain Computer Company's VideoBrain, one of the first consumer computers to be developed.

VideoBrain

Billed as the first family computer, VideoBrain is the brainchild of David Chung, an electronics engineer who headed the engineering team at Fairchild Camera and Instrument that developed that firm's F8 microprocessor. Chung's philosophy about personal computers is that few people are willing to learn programming to use a computer.

His VideoBrain computer eliminates the need to understand a computer language with the help of solid-state program cartridges that are simply inserted into the computer. Each cartridge contains a prerecorded program ROM (read-only memory) that guides the user through a game, checkbook balancing routine, or other task with straightforward English words and phrases flashed on the screen of a home television set connected to the computer.

"The consumer is accustomed to buying books, records and preprogrammed music tape cassettes rather than writing or recording his own. Now he can do the same with VideoBrain program cartridges," according to Chung.

Despite its apparent simplicity when compared with more sophisticated appliance computers such as the Commodore PET and Radio Shack's TRS-80, Video-Brain includes several advanced features. It's housed in a console that incorporates a built-in, modified, typewriter-style keyboard. The placement and staggered arrangement of letters on the keyboard is identical to that of a conventional typewriter. Unfortunately, there are no separate keys for the digits 0 through 9 as on a standard typewriter or microcomputer keyboard. Instead, the 10 digits (and various other symbols and punctuation marks) form secondary functions on various keys. This means that the shift key must be pressed at the same time a digit key is pressed.

VideoBrain's most impressive feature is its color graphics capability. The computer can be attached to a color television and produce up to 16 colors on its screen. Thanks to a proprietary process developed by VideoBrain, very high resolution graphics are possible. A TV game, for example, can produce approximately 80 picture elements across the width of a television screen. The VideoBrain process produces 180 picture elements across the screen for a total of approximately 100,000 elements over the entire screen.

The result of this enhanced resolution enables

VideoBrain to produce very realistic games in full color. There are program cartridges, for example, that place a checkerboard, blackjack game, and even a pinball machine on a TV screen.

VideoBrain is supplied with two joysticks, AC adapter, TV hookup cable, and an introductory program cartridge. Several peripherals are also available, including a cassette interface system dubbed Expander 1. An acoustic coupler called Expander 2 permits VideoBrain to communicate with other computers by means of an ordinary telephone.

VideoBrain is not nearly as powerful a machine as the PET or TRS-80. Nevertheless, its price without a video monitor is comparable to the TRS-80. Another major drawback is the $29.95-plus price of program cartridges.

According to the VideoBrain Computer Company, developing a program cartridge requires up to six months and costs between $25,000 and $50,000. Each cartridge contains a program developed by one or more experts who receive a royalty based on sales. Following extensive testing and modification, each program is stored in a ROM memory chip contained in the program cartridge.

Though the use of cartridges provides a very simple approach to using a computer, it permits no user modification to the program. Appliance computers like the PET and TRS-80 can process thousands of different BASIC programs, many of which are available free. The user must manually enter such programs by typing them into the computer's keyboard, but he can then transfer them to cassette tape for quick and easy retrieval anytime he wishes to use them, and for considerably less money than VideoBrain's preprogrammed cartridges.

In short, VideoBrain is for those with a healthy budget who want the use of a relatively limited personal computer without having to learn any programming techniques or languages whatsoever.

Appliance Computers

Appliance computers resemble consumer micros in that both kinds of machines are supplied ready to use. Appliance computers, however, are considerably more sophisticated.

An appliance-level micro is a fully programmable, general-purpose machine that understands BASIC or some other higher-level computer language. Indeed, today's appliance computer is in many ways as sophisticated as the biggest and most advanced computers of a decade ago.

Earlier, many of the considerations that apply to the selection of any kind of personal computer were covered in the form of three questionnaire-style checklists. There are a number of additional considerations that apply to appliance computers. They include:

1. Programs and other information typed into an appliance computer are stored in user-accessible RAM memory integrated circuits. How much RAM is supplied with the computer (4K bytes is a reasonable minimum; 8K bytes or more is better)?

2. The connections to the various sections of a computer are arranged in a row of wires or printed circuit conductors called a bus. Which bus does the computer use and how many peripherals are available for connection to the bus?

3. Does the computer use a well-known, higher-level language like BASIC?

4. Is the language permanently stored in a ROM memory, or must it be loaded into the computer's RAM memory from a cassette tape or perforated paper tape when the computer is turned on?

5. Does the computer have sockets for additional memory and circuit cards?

With these and the considerations listed earlier in mind, see if you can identify the relative advantages and disadvantages of three appliance computers described next.

Commodore PET

A few years ago, Commodore Business Machines, Inc., startled the personal computing industry by announcing the arrival of the PET, a complete home computer for $495. Shortly thereafter, the company increased the price of a PET with 4K of user-accessible RAM to $595, and an 8K version for $795. Even at the higher price levels, orders began flowing in and Commodore officials spoke of doing $50 million of PET business in their first year. Unfortunately, assorted production delays and the flood of orders prevented Commodore from meeting its projected delivery schedules. Some customers waited months before receiving their PETs. And, Commodore ceased production of the less expensive 4K PET and turned its attention solely to the more profitable 8K version. For a time, the company also required advance payment for all PETs, even

The PET, made by Commodore Business Machines, Inc.

though a firm delivery date could not be promised. These and other PET-related problems resulted in a major controversy.

Complaints and problems notwithstanding, PET remains one of the most important appliance computers available. The machine uses a 6502 microprocessor, the chip that forms the brain of such popular microcomputers as the Apple II and the single board KIM-1.

The 6502 is a product of MOS Technology. When Commodore decided to enter the personal computing business, they decided not only to use the 6502 but to buy MOS Technology. This vertical integration allows Commodore to produce a computer using its own memory and microprocessor chips without having to depend on outside suppliers. Even more importantly, owning MOS Technology gives Commodore access to the talented engineering team that designed the 6502 and the KIM.

PET's most striking feature is its appearance. It is housed in a futuristic, self-contained console complete with keyboard, nine-inch black and white video monitor, and cassette tape recorder. There are no cables to untangle and connect, and PET is ready to operate as soon as its power cord has been plugged into a household wall outlet. Unfortunately, however, only minimal operating information is supplied with the PET.

Experienced computer users immediately notice two impressive features of PET during an introductory session at the keyboard. The first of these is its very powerful BASIC capability. Designed for Commodore by Microsoft, the software company that developed the BASIC used by the ALTAIR 8800, PET BASIC is stored in 8K of ROM and is instantly available when the computer is turned on. It includes all of the features common to other personal computer BASICs, including direct memory access (PEEK and POKE), the trigonometric functions, strings, arrays, and a real time clock. In case you're not familiar with the jargon of BASIC, you can refer back to the previous chapter for explanations of these and other terms. For now, just accept that the PET has a very complete BASIC capability.

The second impressive aspect of PET is its graphics capability. "Graphics" is the term used to describe the ability to make graphs, drawings, diagrams, and game illustrations on the screen of a computer. The graphics available on PET are unique in that almost every key has a graphic symbol. These symbols, which are stored in the PET's internal ROMs along with the letters of the alphabet, the decimal digits, and various punctuation marks, include lines, bars, arcs, circles, blocks, grids, angles, and even the playing card symbols for the ace, diamond, spade, and heart. Each symbol occupies the same space as an upper case letter of the alphabet. Pressing "SHIFT" and then any symbol key flashes the requested symbol on the screen.

Its outstanding graphics features make PET ideal for many applications ranging from illustrated games and bar graphs of financial data to tabulated tables and teaching trigonometry. If graphics is your principal interest, you should see a live demonstration of the PET.

Although PET's BASIC and graphics features are excellent, its keyboard is not well designed. Most hobby and appliance micros that have a full ASCII keyboard (upper- and possibly lower-case alphabet, the digits 0 through 9, punctuation marks, and various symbols) use a conventional typewriter-style keyboard. This greatly simplifies the introduction of a computer system to a beginner. And, it means that a touch-typist can shift between a conventional typewriter and a computer keyboard without having to resort to the slow, frustrating, and inefficient "hunt and peck" method.

So what's wrong with PET's keyboard? It's more like an oversize calculator keyboard than the keyboard of a typewriter. The keys are close together with key-to-key spacing only about two-thirds that of a typewriter's keys, and the keys are not staggered; instead, they are arranged in a flat, rectangular format. Furthermore, the keys have very little "feel" (tactile feedback in computer jargon) , and some users have complained that the symbols on the key tops tend to wear off with use.

Perhaps Commodore will eventually remedy PET's keyboard problems, but present PET owners will have to be satisfied with a less-than-desirable input mechanism. Nevertheless, even with its keyboard, the superb graphics and BASIC capabilities of the PET make it an exceptionally powerful appliance computer.

Radio Shack TRS-80

During all the ballyhoo that accompanied the arrival of the PET, Radio Shack surprised everybody by quietly introducing its personal computer. While Commodore issued statements explaining delivery delays and pricing policies, Radio Shack accepted orders and delivered computers.

Emphasizing its dedication to personal computing, Radio Shack's parent corporation, Tandy Corporation, has begun a subsidiary called Tandy Computers. This new firm operates computer stores in several major cities with additional stores planned for the future. In addition to the TRS-80 and its peripherals, Tandy Computers sells personal computers and peripherals, electronic parts, computer books and magazines, and other products commonly found in computer stores.

Though the TRS-80 has not been the subject of controversy, Radio Shack's promotion of TRS-80-based business computer systems has been strongly criticized. Most critics complain that the TRS-80-based business computer is far too weak to support anything more than trivial business applications, at least as presently configured.

The TRS-80 is a very compact computer. All the electronics, including the Z80 microprocessor, up to 16K of user-accessible RAM, and either 4K or 12K of ROM containing Radio Shack's Level-I or Level-II BASIC are installed on a single circuit board mounted behind the unit's typewriter-style keyboard. The overall dimensions are 16-1/2 by 8 by 3-1/2 inches.

The small size of the TRS-80 is somewhat deceiving, however, because it must be connected either to a modified television set or to Radio Shack's TRS-80 12-inch video monitor before it can be used. Since few people are sufficiently skilled to make the requisite modifications to enable the TRS-80 to be connected to a TV, almost all users opt for Radio Shack's monitor.

Whether the TRS-80 is connected to a video monitor or to a modified TV, it's necessary to use a special cable to complete the link between computer and display terminal. Depending on where you plan to use a computer, this may or may not be a disadvantage. It's obviously a drawback when portability is required; it makes little or no difference when the computer is intended for use in a fixed location.

Unlike the PET, the TRS-80 does not include a built-in cassette recorder. As with the monitor, this means external cables must be used to connect a recorder to the computer.

Again, this may or may not be a major drawback. On the positive side, you can use a recorder you already own with the TRS-80. If the computer will be used at one principal location, the connection cables should be no problem. On the negative side, portability is not a virtue of a TRS-80 plus monitor and recorder. All these items can be carried, but the most practical and certainly the safest way to transport the system is to disconnect the peripherals and then make two trips or get some help.

The TRS-80's 53-key ASCII keyboard (upper-case characters only) is almost identical in format to that of the industry standard, IBM's Selectric typewriter. Some symbols and punctuation marks, however, are in different locations, and there are several new symbols and functions (for editing, graphics, etc.). The keyboard also has good "feel," and touch-typists readily adapt to it.

As noted earlier, the TRS-80 is available with either Level-I or Level-II BASIC in ROM. Being in ROM means that the language is permanent, even with electric power off. Even by personal computer standards, Level-I BASIC is considered relatively weak. It does not include such powerful features as strings and arrays. Editing of programs is painstaking. And the only mathematical functions accessible directly from the keyboard are add, subtract, multiply, and divide.

Of course, subroutines that derive such useful items as square root, logarithms, and various trigonometric functions can be stored in RAM and called into action when needed. But this is awkward, time-consuming, and inefficient because the subroutines must be reloaded each time the TRS-80 is turned on. Furthermore, they use up valuable memory space.

In sum, Level-I BASIC is about as effective as a $10 pocket calculator when it comes to arithmetic. Any good scientific calculator can easily outperform Level-I

Radio Shack's TRS-80 system.

BASIC in solving complex mathematical problems. It does have provisions for limited graphics, though. And, with the company's packaged cassettes, it presents backgammon and blackjack games on a TV screen.

Fortunately, many of Level-I BASIC's weaknesses are corrected by Level II. Mathematical functions, for example, include square root, sine, cosine, tangent, logarithm, and various others. Of interest to serious programmers and anyone else primarily concerned about the communication ability of a computer, Level-II BASIC includes such powerful features as strings and arrays.

Strings allow you to write programs that permit you to communicate with the computer using ordinary English words and phrases. Arrays permit a computer to organize large amounts of information (checkbook figures, inventory, record collection, etc.) in an efficient manner.

In short, Level-II BASIC is far superior to Level I. Unlike Commodore, which dropped its PET with 4K BASIC when it perfected the 8K version, Radio Shack sells the TRS-80 with Level I or Level II. And, Level-I customers can later upgrade their computers to Level II for about $100, a more than reasonable price considering the additional capability that results.

Another aspect of the TRS-80 that you should know about concerns the range of peripherals that are available. One of the most interesting and important is the TRS-80 Expansion Interface, a cabinet-like enclosure that can be attached to the bottom of the TRS-80 video monitor. It contains sockets for an additional 16K or 32K of user-accessible RAM memory and circuitry that permits the TRS-80 Mini-Disk Drive floppy disk to be connected to the TRS-80. It also contains a real time clock and circuits for connecting a printer, additional cassette recorder (for a total of two), and a teletypewriter to the TRS-80.

Radio Shack's TRS-80 Mini-Disk Drive stores 80K bytes on a single mini-floppy disk. The average time required to find a particular bit of information stored on a disk is about half a second. The disk drive requires a TRS-80 computer with 16K of RAM memory, Level-II BASIC, and the Expansion Interface.

Radio Shack sells two kinds of printers for the TRS-80. The TRS-80 Screen Printer is an ultra-fast electrostatic printer that spews out the entire contents of the video display, including graphics, in under a second when a single print button is touched. The cost is about the same as a 4K TRS-80 plus video display. The screen printer requires only 4K of RAM and Level-I BASIC so that it can be connected directly to the standard 4K TRS-80.

The TRS-80 Line Printer is available for about twice the cost of the TRS-80 Screen Printer. It impact prints from 60 to 110 characters per second using a matrix of 35 dots arranged in the usual 5 by 7-inch format. Since this printer prints on standard roll paper (up to 9.8 inches wide) , and since its print density can be adjusted from 10 to 16.5 characters per inch, the TRS-80 Line Printer can be used for small business applications. It requires a standard TRS-80 with 4K of RAM, Level-II BASIC, and the Expansion Interface.

While these are the principal TRS-80 peripherals available from Radio Shack, several small electronics companies have already announced various other devices, particularly circuit boards, that can be connected to the TRS-80 bus. One will permit the TRS-80 to be connected to the many boards that have been developed for the popular S-100 bus.

Apple II

One of the first console-style personal computers with a built-in keyboard is the Apple II. Introduced by the Apple Computer Company in 1977, Apple II is a more sophisticated appliance version of the earlier Apple I single board computer. Apple I itself was a significant product because it was one of the first hobby computers to include the video display circuits, microprocessor, power supply, and memory integrated circuits on a single printed circuit board.

Apple II is significantly more expensive than either the PET or TRS-80. And, it does not include a video display. Instead, it is designed to be connected to any standard black and white or color television set by means of a low-cost modulator circuit that is attached to the TV's antenna terminals. Probably because it requires FCC approval, a time-consuming and sometimes costly requirement, this modulator is not supplied by the Apple Computer Company. Instead, the firm recommends outside sources who manufacture FCC-approved modulators.

These disadvantages are very significant. Nevertheless, the Apple II has attracted considerable interest,

Apple Computer Company's Apple II.

particularly among traditional computer hobbyists. One of the principal reasons for all this interest is Apple II's impressive color graphics capability. While the graphics are not nearly as flexible or complete as those of the PET, color opens up a new dimension to even limited graphics. Relatively simple BASIC instructions can be used to produce graphics and text in up to 15 different colors.

Color graphics make possible a wide variety of computer games, and Apple II's designers have capitalized on this by allowing hand-operated joysticks to be connected directly to the computer. Two are included with the standard Apple II. A built-in speaker permits various sound effects that will be controlled by software to be produced.

The standard Apple II comes with 4K of user-accessible RAM. Integrated circuit sockets on the computer's circuit board permit additional integrated circuits to be plugged in by a computer store salesman or even the machine's owner. This means that up to 44K of RAM can be added to the 4K already present.

The standard Apple II includes 8K bytes of ROM, 6K of which contains Apple's version of BASIC. Apple Computer Corporation does not make a printer or video monitor for the Apple II, but a variety of peripherals are planned. These include circuit boards for music synthesis, two types of boards that allow the computer to be connected to external devices, and a power controller that allows the computer to switch lights and appliances connected to 110-volt household line current on and off.

According to the company, the addition of one or more of these peripherals will allow the Apple II to monitor home heating and cooling systems, smoke detectors, and burglar alarms. The computer can also be programmed to turn on lights in a home in an apparently random manner to give the illusion that the home is occupied when the owner is away. Some of these applications, it should be noted, require modifications to home wiring.

With 12K of RAM, Apple II can generate a high resolution graphic display in up to four colors. In this mode the video screen is divided into 280 by 192 display points.

While graphics, particularly color graphics, are nice, the prospective purchaser of a personal computer must carefully compare the benefits of graphics with their cost. The standard Apple II without monitor costs more than twice as much as the TRS-80 with monitor and cassette recorder!

Are color graphics worth the difference? If you're interested in developing novel computer displays for business and educational applications, the answer might very well be yes. If your principal interest is games, perhaps you should look at some of the very capable and much cheaper color TV video game systems that are available.

Comparing Appliance Computers

Of those appliance computers available at this time, Commodore's PET and Radio Shack's TRS-80 domi-

	PET	TRS-80
Standard Keyboard	No	Yes
BASIC	Excellent	Level I-weak
		Level II-excellent
Video Monitor	Built-in	Cable-connected
Maximum Memory	32K	64K
Graphics	Excellent	Fair
Cassette Interface	Built-in Cassette	Cable-connected Recorder
Printer Available	Yes	Yes
Disk Drive Available	No	Yes
Documentation (Instruction Manual, etc.)	Weak	Good

nate the market. Since these two computers no doubt foreshadow the trend of appliance-level personal computers in coming years, their key features and specifications are compared on page 211.

Hobby Computers

Personal computing began with the advent of do-it-yourself kit computers. The building experience provides considerable knowledge about the hardware aspects of a computer and enables the user to perform at least some of his own servicing. Also, a wide range of peripherals has been developed for the hobby computer market. Moreover, building your own can save you money, though this isn't always necessarily true.

If you are seriously interested in the hardware aspects of personal computing, you might want to consider assembling your own micro. Or, you might want to purchase a preassembled, single board computer to gain firsthand experience in programming a micro using machine language. A few points about machine language will be covered later in this chapter.

All the hardware, software, and general considerations that were discussed earlier apply to hobby computers. Many of the appliance computer considerations also apply.

Here, however, are some additional factors that you should consider when evaluating competing hobby level micros:

1. If the computer is a kit, is it accompanied by detailed, step-by-step assembly instructions that include pictorial representations of key assembly steps?

2. Is it possible to purchase a copy of the assembly manual prior to making a purchase so that you can judge both your ability to assemble the kit and the quality of the instructions?

3. Does the manufacturer offer kit assembly advice should you encounter a major obstacle?

4. Does the manufacturer provide service for customer-assembled computer kits?

5. How does the cost of the kit computer compare with a preassembled appliance micro with comparable features and capabilities?

6. If a preassembled appliance computer with similar features and capabilities is available for about the same price as a kit hobby computer, what significant advantages, if any, will result from buying the kit computer?

7. If you are thinking about buying a single board micro to gain firsthand experience with machine language programming, is the computer that you are considering supplied ready to operate? Or, is it necessary for you to supply a power supply, video monitor, and other key components?

Be sure to keep all these considerations in mind as you study about representative hobby computers. Also, remember that the computers described are merely representative of more than two dozen different kinds of hobby and single board micros now available. For information about other hobby computers, visit your local computer store or see recent issues of a personal computing magazine.

Processor Technology Corp. SOL-20

After *Popular Electronics* magazine introduced the first hobby computer, the ALTAIR 8800, in its January 1975 issue, several small spin-off or "parasite" companies were soon established to produce circuit boards that could be used with the machine. One of these small companies was the Processor Technology Corporation.

In July 1976, *Popular Electronics* published a construction article about an intelligent computer terminal that had almost as much impact as the ALTAIR. Designed by Processor Technology and named for the magazine's technical editor, Leslie Solomon, SOL had something that the ALTAIR did not—a typewriter-style keyboard integrated with the main frame computer into a neat package. This meant that programs and other information could be entered directly into a computer without having to use a row of toggle switches found on the ALTAIR or using a separate, space-taking keyboard assembly.

SOL was a big hit with magazine readers, and 18 months after the construction article appeared more than 5000 were said to have been sold.

Today, Processor Technology has become a major hobby computer manufacturer. SOL has evolved into SOL-20, an 8080 microprocessor-based small computer. SOL-20 is housed in an attractive blue metal case with walnut side panels. The case is fitted with a

Processor Technology's SOL-20 computer.

self-contained 85-key upper- and lower-case keyboard plus a separate calculator-style keyboard for quick entry of numbers.

SOL-20 includes a 1024-character video display circuit that permits the computer to be connected to a video monitor or a modified television set. The single circuit board in the SOL-20 console also includes a built-in audio cassette tape interface and an interchangeable plug-in ROM memory card called a "personality module." Three personality modules are available. The SOLOS module optimizes SOL for use as a small computer. The SOLED module enables SOL to function as an electronic text editor or word processor. The CONSOL module, the simplest of the three, enables SOL to function as a very basic computer terminal.

The SOL-20 circuit board has only 1024 bytes of RAM memory available for program storage but additional memory modules can be added. Since BASIC 5, a simplified form of BASIC designed by Processor Technology, requires a minimum RAM capacity of 8K bytes, a prospective SOL-20 purchaser should add the cost of this additional memory to the projected cost of a complete computer. A more powerful 8K BASIC requires a minimum of 12K bytes of RAM.

SOL-20 is available in kit form or factory assembled. The price, even for the kit version, is higher than that of the ready-to-use TRS-80.

One of the principal attributes of the SOL-20 is its S-100 bus. This means that it can be used with the many modules and circuit boards originally developed for the ALTAIR 8800. As one of the first major S-100 spin-off companies, Processor Technology manufactures a number of S-100 compatible modules that can be used with the SOL-20. Up to five S-100 cards can be plugged into the SOL-20 cabinet.

Only experienced kit builders should attempt to assemble a kit version of the SOL-20. One builder with a college degree in engineering physics required 36 hours to assemble his SOL-10, a slightly simpler version of the SOL-20, and found several construction errors. He then spent five hours finishing the walnut side panels. Another builder required a high-speed oscilloscope to discover several assembly errors and some defective integrated circuits.

Despite these assembly problems, both builders later recommended the SOL computer system in articles that they wrote for personal computing magazines. If you're interested in the SOL system, you might refer to "A User's Reaction to the SOL-10 Computer" (Robert Bumpous, *BYTE,* January 1978, pp. 86-93) and "Fillet of SOL" (Gary Dozier, *Personal Computing,* April 1978, pp. 28-31). For a report by an owner of a preassembled SOL, refer to "User's Report: The SOL-20" (*BYTE,* April 1978, pp. 126-130).

Heathkit H8

The Heath Company is by far the largest and most important manufacturer of electronic do-it-yourself kits. In case you're not familiar with the company's line of Heathkits, they include everything from digital clocks and home weather stations to electronic test equipment and color television sets.

The Heath Company took a long look at the fast

ALTAIR 8800 micro with Soroc CRT terminal and floppy disk drives.

Heathkit's H11 computer, H9 video terminal, and H10 paper tape reader/punch.

moving hobby computer field before making a decision to enter the market. Eventually, the company introduced the H8 computer, an 8080A microprocessor-based system with a 16-key front panel keyboard for manually entering machine language programs. The front panel also includes a digital readout that displays the address of a memory location being loaded with information as well as the information itself (a number or program instruction).

At first glance, the H8 appears to be one of the most reasonably priced hobby computers available. The H8, however, cannot be operated without the addition of at least one H8-1 4K RAM memory board. The financial catch is that the H8 does not include an H8-1 board.

Even dedicated hobby computer enthusiasts soon tire of entering lengthy machine language programs via a limited numeric keyboard. Fortunately, Heath sells the H9, a complete video terminal kit that can be connected to the H8. These two components with the Heathkit H8-5 Cassette Interface and ECP-3801 Cassette Recorder/Player constitute a complete small computer system similar in many respects to an appliance computer like the TRS-80 but costing almost twice as much.

Is the added cost of the Heathkit computer justified? For many prospective home computerists, the answer is no, particularly since many hours are required to assemble the computer before a single program can be executed. The TRS-80 can be connected to its video monitor and both units plugged into a wall outlet and used to process programs as soon as they are removed from the cartons in which they were shipped. For dedicated computer hobbyists, however, the H8 offers several significant advantages over both appliance computers and hobby micros sold by competing kit companies.

The most important of these is Heath's record of reliability and service. Unlike some hobby computer companies that have cast aside the hobbyist market and moved up to the small business market or gone out of business, Heath is dedicated to the electronic hobbyist market. The Heath Company is also well known for excellent customer service. Personal kit-building assistance is available at Heathkit Electronic Centers. For customers who do not reside near a center, Heath has a staff of technical consultants who answer telephone or written requests for assistance in building and operating a kit. Heath will even repair completed kits that do not operate properly, provided no modifications to the kit were attempted.

Another advantage is the quality of the assembly manuals and technical documentation supplied with Heathkit equipment. Assembly manuals provide a complete list of parts and a detailed assembly checklist. Documentation supplied with the H8 is among the best in the hobby computer industry.

Still another advantage of a Heathkit micro is a full line of peripherals that readily interface with the H8. In addition to the H9 Video Terminal, peripherals available so far include the H10 Paper Tape Reader/Punch Kit for storing programs and data on paper tape, the

H27 Floppy Drive disk memory system, and the LA36 DEC Writer II Printer Terminal.

What do users of the H8 have to say about it? One who happens to be a microcomputer expert was impressed with several hardware aspects of the machine, but he was critical of the H8's limited numerical range. For example, the machine cannot perform the almost trivial problem of balancing a checkbook with a balance in excess of $9999.99. He also noted that the

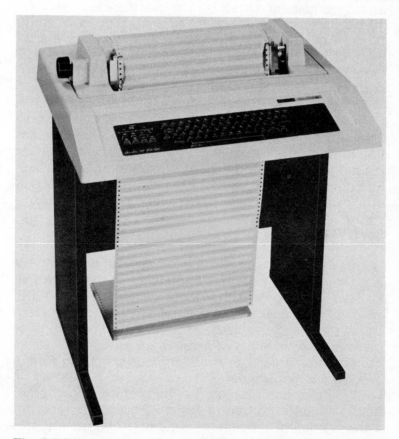

The DEC Writer II keyboard printer terminal.

H8's video terminal uses more than 100 integrated circuits, far more than a more efficient design would have required (a new terminal reportedly is being developed).

Incidentally, ambitious computer hobbyists with a pocketful of money should have a look at the Heathkit / DEC H11 Computer. Most microcomputers, hobby and otherwise, are 8-bit machines. The H11 is a 16-bit computer, and this gives it capabilities that are in some ways superior to 8-bit micros.

Though the H11 is a kit, the key portion of the system is supplied as a fully assembled and tested circuit board containing an LS1-11 microprocessor and 4K 16-bit words of memory. This board is a product of the Digital Equipment Corporation (DEC), a major manufacturer of commercial computers. It makes the H11 functionally equivalent to the PDP 11, a very popular—and costly—minicomputer made by DEC.

Through a licensing agreement between Heath Company and Digital Equipment Corporation, purchasers of the H11 are provided with a generous selection of software (on paper tape), including the higher languages BASIC and FOCAL. Developed by the Digital Equipment Corporation, FOCAL is designed for scientific, mathematical, and engineering applications.

SWTPC 6800

Southwest Technical Products Corporation (SWTPC) is a firm with considerable experience in the electronic kit field. Long before the debut of the ALTAIR 8800, SWTPC was selling audio amplifier kits, digital electronics learning modules, and various other kinds of electronics kits. Many of these kits were introduced as construction articles in *Popular Electronics* and *Radio-Electronics* magazines.

SWTPC's contribution to the personal computer field is the 6800 computer system. This computer is not a true "system" since it consists only of a central processing unit, memory boards and a power supply in-

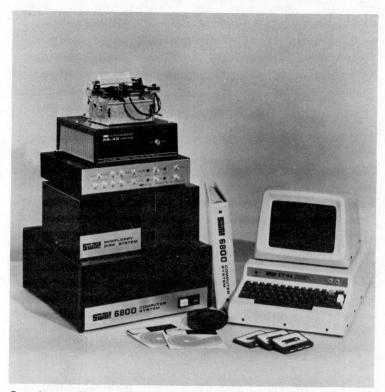

Southwest Technical Products Corporation's 6800 computer system with peripherals.

stalled in a metal cabinet with no input or output facilities. The only controls are a power switch and a reset switch, so that the 6800 can be used only after it's been connected to an input-output terminal such as a Teletype ASR-33 or SWTPC's CT-64 terminal system. The CT-64, which is also a kit, has a built-in typewriter keyboard and a cathode ray tube video monitor that can display 16 lines with either 32 or 64 characters per line. All ASCII characters (including the lower-case alphabet) can be displayed with the CT-64.

The 6800 computer is easily expanded since all the

circuit boards are inserted into receptacles mounted on a 9 by 14-inch mother board installed in the bottom of the computer's cabinet. The mother board will accept the computer's CPU board, up to four memory boards (for a total storage capacity of 32K bytes), and two additional boards. Additional boards can be connected to the computer by adding a second mother board.

The SWTPC 6800 was the first major hobby computer to depart from the S-100 bus of the ALTAIR 8800. Instead, the 6800 uses a more compact SS-50 bus that has only half the number of conductors.

The 6800 computer is definitely for experienced kit builders only. The assembly instructions do not take the hand-holding approach used by Heath. A brochure on the 6800 explains the company's philosophy about kit building:

> Another thing we would like to make clear is that our computer systems and terminal systems are sold in kit form only. We do not offer them in assembled form. Our instructions have been written for the individual who has built up electronic projects before, knows how to recognize the various components, and is experienced at printed circuit board soldering. Although the instructions include step-by-step assembly details, schematics, pictorials, wiring diagrams, and a theory of operation, they have not been written for the beginner. The various modules within each of the kits simply plug together keeping the wiring to a minimum.

If you're an experienced kit builder, the 6800 has several important advantages over its competitors. For one, SWTPC is an established kit company that delivers what it promises within a reasonable time.

Additionally, SWTPC offers a complete line of peripherals, including a dual floppy disk (MF-68), audio cassette interface (AC-30), alphanumeric printer (PR-

40), graphics terminal (GT-61), and a potentiometer digitizer (joystick). They also sell a series of SS-50 circuit cards that are designed to be plugged into the 6800 mother board. These include various memory boards, several input/output boards designed to interface the computer with various external peripherals, and a calculator interface board that allows the 6800 to perform arithmetic without using BASIC or some other higher-level language.

Software for the 6800 includes both 4K and 8K BASIC on cassette tape, paper tape or a floppy disk. Note that BASIC is not stored in a ROM. Before the 6800 can be used to process programs written in BASIC, the BASIC interpreter must first be loaded into the computer's memory. While this is a disadvantage to some users, it means that interpreters for languages other than BASIC can be loaded into the computer's memory. That makes the 6800 clumsier to use but much more flexible than a machine with BASIC in ROM.

COSMAC VIP

RCA's COSMAC VIP is one of about a dozen single board microcomputers. Most single board computers were originally designed to permit engineers, students, and hobbyists to become acquainted with a particular company's microprocessor. The various microprocessors that are available differ in many respects, and one of the fastest ways to learn how to use and apply one is with the help of a single board computer based on a particular microprocessor.

The COSMAC VIP uses RCA's CDP1802 microprocessor, a CMOS device that consumes very little electrical power. Though engineers and other specialists will find the COSMAC VIP a handy way to become familiar with the CDP1802, RCA bills the VIP as a hobby computer.

The COSMAC VIP includes 2K bytes of user-accessible RAM, a cassette tape recorder interface circuit, sound effects circuits, and a built-in calculator-type keyboard for entering programs.

Most single board computers include several LED readouts that display the address of a memory location being loaded with information as well as the information. The information can be a number or a machine language program instruction. The COSMAC VIP, however, has no LED readouts. Instead, the computer is designed to be connected to an RCA nine-inch video display monitor. This is made possible by a special video display integrated circuit.

The assembled version of the COSMAC VIP is housed in a plastic console that leaves the keyboard exposed and incorporates a speaker (for programmed sound effects), four empty integrated circuit sockets that will accept memory chips containing an additional 2K bytes of user-accessible RAM, one input and one output terminal (or port) to allow the computer to con-

RCA's COSMAC VIP single-board microcomputer.

trol or be controlled by an external device, and two sockets for adding additional circuit boards to the computer.

Like other single board computers, the COSMAC VIP provides the least expensive way of getting into personal computing. But don't rush out and buy the VIP (or any other single board micro) before giving some consideration to a major drawback: single board computers must be programmed with the machine language of the microprocessor they use. This means a lengthy and tedious entry of hexadecimal numbers, like AF, 1E, 64, 7F, FF, 12, 37..., into the calculator-style keyboard. The hexadecimal numbers represent both program instructions and numerical data.

A more significant problem is the availability of suitable software. You can write your own programs, of course, but learning and understanding enough machine language to write even reasonably interesting and useful programs is difficult and time-consuming.

Some programs are supplied by manufacturers and others are available from computer books, magazines and various user's clubs that have been formed. Nevertheless, finding software for single board computers can still be a major problem.

With all these drawbacks, why should a computer hobbyist even consider acquiring a single board computer like the COSMAC VIP?

Besides a reasonably low cost (about $250), a single board computer offers an outstanding educational opportunity to learn about the innermost workings of a microcomputer. Experience with a single board micro can be an excellent training ground for a hobbyist who wants to pursue computer science or electronics professionally.

A TRS-80 or PET offers far more computing power for a serious BASIC programmer, but the skeleton-like configuration of a single board computer offers far more opportunity to learn about microcomputer basics.

The Future of Personal Computing

THE DEVELOPMENT of high-technology electronic products for consumers has become a major industry in recent years. Many new and fascinating electronic gadgets are now available. They include wafer-thin calculators that are the size of a business card, solar-powered digital watches with continuously operating liquid crystal displays and assorted stop watch features, and computer-like video games.

Even more amazing consumer electronic products will be introduced in coming years. Even the arrival of the personal computer, possibly the most far-reaching consumer electronic product since television, is considered by some authorities as merely a prelude to what is yet to come.

For example, Robert Wickham, president of Vantage Research, wrote in a recent issue of *Datamation* that "The current crop of personal computer products looks rather frail and primitive in comparison to what is to come."

If you are very serious about personal computing and are thinking about acquiring your own micro, do not let the promise of better things to come have too much influence on your decision to buy a computer now or in a few years. In striking contrast to an otherwise inflation-ravaged market for consumer products, you can now purchase a version of a computer that would have cost more than $25,000 a decade ago for well under $1000. How many other products can boast of a comparable cost reduction?

Whether you decide to purchase your own computer now or later, you should be aware of what's in store for personal computing. The major breakthrough, the arrival of personal computing, has already taken place. But hardware and software developments scheduled for the early 1980s will make personal computing even more fascinating than it already is.

Talking and Listening to a Computer

Many people are convinced that widespread acceptance of personal computing will occur only when users can give orders to computers using ordinary spoken words, and, in turn, receive oral responses from a computer.

Is this expectation a result of the popularity of science fiction television programs and motion pictures? Not at all, for the technology that permits verbal communication with a computer is here today. We've discussed several different circuit boards for hobby computers that use the popular S-100 bus to enable a computer to respond to a limited number of spoken words and synthesize speech. Although these boards can form the basis of some fascinating experiments in oral computer communications, their capabilities are very primitive compared to what will be available in the 1980s.

Consider Interstate Electronics Corporation's Voice Terminal. This system, which is available today, can be "taught" to understand up to 900 different spoken words with a recognition accuracy of more than 99 percent! A vocabulary of this size is ideal for oral computer programming and even limited conversion of speech directly into typewritten form.

At $20,000, the cost of the Voice Terminal is far out of the personal computer price range, but it's safe to say that the development of new electronics technology will eventually reduce the cost of practical computer voice input mechanisms to a few hundred dollars. Skeptical? Then consider that a video terminal with less capability than Radio Shack's TRS-80 computer cost as much as $20,000 in 1968!

Will computers of the future be able to talk? We described Speech Plus, a circuit board that gives a robot-like voice to a micro with an S-100 bus. Recently, Texas Instruments introduced a sophisticated learning toy that features a 200-word vocabulary stored in solid-state memory chips. The "toy" is intended to help children learn to spell.

With developments such as these, it is not difficult to envision a personal computer that responds to spoken instructions with spoken replies!

More Memory Capacity

The most important memory to the typical personal computer user is the semiconductor RAM integrated circuits that store programs and other temporary information. For mass information storage, the floppy disk memory is the best choice. But, as we said earlier,

RAM memory is relatively expensive and requires a continuous supply of electrical current to retain the information stored within it. Disk memories store individual bits of information for a small fraction of a penny, but a typical disk memory system for a personal computer costs $500 or more. That's why so many personal computer users use low-cost cassette tape.

The prices for semiconductor RAMs, however, drop each year, and it's likely that personal computers of the 1980s will use far more RAM memory than today's micros for about the same price. This will result in much more powerful computers and reduce the need for saving memory space with painstaking programming methods.

As for mass storage, the expensive floppy disk memory system will receive strong competition from the bubble memory. By the early 1980s, bubble memories with a storage capacity of a million or more bits will be available. They'll likely be cheaper and much smaller than disk memories. And, unlike RAMs, they will retain information permanently without requiring a continuous flow of electrical current.

Handheld Computers

One of the most exciting personal computer developments expected in the 1980s will be handheld microcomputers. Advanced, handheld programmable calculators available today, such as Texas Instruments' TI-59 and Hewlett-Packard's HP-67, possess many computer-like features. But the handheld calculator of the next decade will be even more advanced.

In the next few years, you can expect to see handheld calculators with "user-definable keyboards" and alphanumeric displays. User-definable keyboards will permit an operator to assign any function or operation to any key on the keyboard. The result will be a customized calculator. Alphanumeric readouts will permit calculators to display letters and words.

Advanced calculators of the future will also probably be capable of interfacing with various kinds of peripherals such as printers, memory modules, magnetic card readers, and other devices.

One of the major technical limitations in attempting to design a true handheld computer is the readout. If you've had an opportunity to use a micro, you already know how helpful it is to see a series of lines that you've typed into the unit's keyboard on the video display. Can the video display's cathode ray tube (CRT) be miniaturized to a size where it can fit in a handheld calculator case? Not likely. But other display methods may be able to replace the CRT in a handheld computer.

One possibility is the power-saving liquid crystal display, the type used in many new calculators and digital watches. Already several companies make miniature liquid crystal screens that can display several rows of characters, symbols and words much like a miniature, flat-screen CRT. Perhaps this new display technology will permit the development of a truly personal, handheld computer during the 1980s.

Attaching Micros to Telephones

For years, computers have been able to communicate with one another over ordinary telephone lines. Even today, some personal computer enthusiasts play games and exchange programs and other information with computers located miles away. They do this by using their own micro as a remote terminal capable of sending and receiving information to and from the distant computer.

Computers can be connected directly to telephone lines, but the telephone company must approve the connection and may require that a special interface circuit be placed between the computer and the line to protect telephone company equipment. A way around this problem is to use a peripheral called an acoustically coupled modem. Modem means modulate-demodulate. You can think of a modem as a device that converts computer information into sound and reconverts sound into computer information.

An acoustic coupler is nothing more than a microphone and speaker that is installed in a small housing into which a telephone handset can be placed. With the help of a pair of acoustic couplers and modems, two computers can literally "talk" to one another using ordinary telephones!

How will the future of personal computing be affected by the ability to connect micros to telephone lines? The possibilities are quite exciting. For example, consider electronic mail. With the rising price of postage, the prospect of electronic mail is more a question of when than how. The technology for electronic mail, of course, is here today. Just ask any personal computer owner who has an acoustically coupled modem and a printer connected to his micro.

Many future applications for micros connected to telephone lines will make little or no use of the machine's computing abilities. Instead, the micro will simply serve as a communications terminal.

One application will be using a modem-equipped micro to request information from a distant library capable of receiving and processing electronic inquiries. Another will provide direct access to a person's account records at a bank.

No doubt you can think of other applications for a micro connected to a telephone. How about a convenient communications method for deaf persons? Or, perhaps, a way of checking up on your house security while you're away on vacation with a quick phone call to your computer!

More and Better Software

If personal computer owners, manufacturers and magazines agree on any one topic, it is the lack of good, quality software. Software, as you'll recall, is computer jargon for the programs that tell computers what to do and how to do it. Although there is more than a decade of accumulated BASIC software—more than enough to keep the typical personal computer owner busy for years to come—there have been no major break-throughs in BASIC programming since the language was invented. This is in sharp contrast to the incredible size and cost reductions in computer hardware that have occurred during the same period.

Will the advent of personal computing bring with it an era of more and better software? Many observers think that may very well happen. They note that personal computing has expanded the number of computer programmers to the tens of thousands.

Many micro users and owners are young high school and university students who are full of new ideas, unencumbered by traditional approaches to programming, and therefore open to new and highly creative approaches to software. It is possible that vast quantities of new and improved software will flow from the keyboards of these new computer enthusiasts in coming years. Perhaps one or more gifted personal computer enthusiasts will invent a new programming language that will greatly simplify the use of personal computers, thus opening up the field of personal computing to an even wider audience.

More Advanced Programming Languages

Imagine a programming language that would allow you to type the following message into the keyboard of a personal computer:

"Print the square of the numbers from 1 to 100."

A simple statement like this would replace the following BASIC program:

```
10 FOR X = TO 100
20 PRINT X * X
30 NEXT X
```

Obviously the first program is the simplest of the two. It's also the easiest to use with a computer that understands spoken commands. Even better, the first program is already a reality, thanks to new developments in advanced programming languages.

Until new conversational programming languages are perfected, BASIC will remain the most popular programming language for personal computers. BASIC is relatively easy to learn and tens of thousands of personal computers with BASIC stored in ready-to-use solid-state memory chips are now in use.

But despite its popularity, BASIC's days as the most popular language for personal computers are numbered. Futuristic computers that understand spoken words and phrases will require the conversational programming languages much like the example we've just discussed.

New conversational-style programming languages are now being developed by several universities and computer companies. Even personal computer users are in the act. Several have come up with their own versions of advanced conversational programming languages.

A Computer in Every Home?

The predictions about new hardware and software for personal computers that we've just examined are all based on either what is currently available in the realm of scientific and industrial computers or what is now undergoing development. While these predictions are all quite reasonable, no doubt you've read some less reasonable predictions about the coming "computer generation." One common prophecy is "a computer in every home."

Rosy predictions about the future of personal computing are often a product of an overzealous press agent or advertising copywriter. While consumer products that use microprocessors will become very common, true personal computers, the kind that have input keyboards and video terminals, will remain a specialty product for quite some time.

Since press releases don't always explain the differences between a true personal computer and a microprocessor-controlled game or appliance, let's identify a few.

As you'll recall, a computer can be made by combining a microprocessor with some memory. Therefore, it is technically correct to say that microprocessor-equipped games, microwave ovens, washing machines, and other consumer products are "computer controlled." But since the programs stored in the memories of these simple computers cannot be changed by their user, they are more accurately referred to as "controllers" or "dedicated computers." For example, a pocket calculator is technically a computer since it contains a microprocessor and memory. But, because a calculator is designed for performing calculations, it is best described as a computer dedicated to calculating. Be sure to keep these distinctions between true personal computers and microprocessor-controlled games and appliances in mind when you read predictions.

Some down-to-earth personal computer experts have taken a hard look at the future of personal computing. They have concluded that micros made with today's hardware and designed to handle today's software simply will not appeal to all consumers. As Lou Frenzel, director of marketing for the Heath Company, observed in the first issue of *Computer Dealer,* "The consumer is simply not ready."

He goes on to note that few consumers know how to program, there are not enough practical applications for very widespread use of personal micros, and many consumers don't have enough motivation to learn to use a personal computer.

Still, Frenzel and other experts who share his views, are confident of a continuing increase in the popularity of personal computing. As more people acquire their own micros, their families and friends will receive an intimate introduction to personal computing. More schools are acquiring computers and providing courses on their use. Computer games can be much more elaborate than the video games that are connected to a TV set. At least one game machine includes "Tiny BASIC" provisions, for example. And less costly hardware and simpler programming languages will encourage more people to become involved in personal computing.

The Personal Computer Technology Gap

Will personal computers create a technology gap between micro users and nonusers? Some observers think such a gap already exists.

One prominent hobby computer expert who recently gave a series of lectures about the technical aspects of microprocessors and personal computers to university electrical engineering students and their professors was stunned to learn that the students knew far more about the subject than their instructors. And, many of the faculty members could not even grasp some of the concepts he described! His conclusion is that a distinct technological gap already exists at the university level.

If some students are able to learn more about the technical side of microcomputing than some of their professors, where does this leave the general public? No doubt many people without technical backgrounds will become interested in personal computing. Many already have. Furthermore, there are computers, such as the VideoBrain, that do not require any programming whatsoever. All programs are simply plugged into the computer. Of course, one is limited to the applications of the company's packaged programs. But for many people, this is sufficient.

Most computers, however, are unlike most consumer products since they require creative action on the part of the operator. They present a challenge, and the person with little or no initiative, or a weak educational background will have a difficult time relating to such a personal computer. As a consequence, personal computer users today are part of an elite group, much as amateur radio operators are. Note, though, that more and more small businesses are using personal computers, giving owners and managers an opportunity to also learn about and use the equipment for personal use.

Future computers that can be programmed using conversational English will permit persons without the desire or ability to learn BASIC to develop their own computer programs. Also computer terminals in the home will open up mass utilization of computers, though it would be a push-button application rather than a creative function. With such a system, a person could shop at a department store, pay a bill, seek and receive information from an encyclopedia, and so on— all done at home. Sound too futuristic? Well, it's already being done in Japan and a few highly industrialized European countries on a small scale.

Until then, personal computing will be largely limited to a highly motivated population of above-average intelligence, with enough money to purchase their own micros and associated equipment, and with enough interest to read books like this one. Indeed, merely reading this book has secured your place in the future of personal computing.

Personal Computer Glossary

ARE YOU confused and bewildered by the strange vocabulary of computer users? This glossary of personal computing terms and "buzz-words" will help you interpret most computer jargon with ease. It includes many terms explained in this book as well as others that you may encounter elsewhere. Become familiar with them and you'll be well-prepared to enter the world of personal computing.

Address: A specific location in a computer's memory that is capable of storing information. Addresses can be identified by binary numbers (machine language) or letters of the alphabet (a higher-level language like BASIC).

Alphanumeric: Information that consists of characters of the alphabet and numbers.

Analog Computer: An electronic or mechanical device that uses a variable quantity, such as a voltage, to represent a numerical quantity. Common examples of simple analog computers include the slide rule, speedometer, and nondigital clock.

Arithmetic Logic Unit: The circuits in the central processing unit that perform arithmetic, and make logical decisions and comparisons in a digital computer.

ASCII Code: An acronym for *American Standard Code for Information Interchange.* ASCII is a binary code for the upper- and lower-case letters of the alphabet, the 10 digits, various punctuation marks, and other symbols. ASCII permits computers to remember and process words as well as numbers.

Assembler: A computer program that transforms the assembly language used by some computers into the binary numbers known as "machine language."

Assembly Language: A computer language representing the binary numbers of the machine language that a computer understands with easily remembered mnemonics (e.g. CLR, LDA, HLT, etc.) that people can understand.

BASIC: An acronym for *Beginner's All-Purpose Symbolic Instruction Code.* BASIC is an easily learned higher-level computer langauge that is used by most personal computer manufacturers.

BCD: A buzzword for Binary Coded Decimal that is a number system used by most calculators and personal computers. BCD assigns the first 10 binary numbers to the 10 decimal digits and permits any decimal number to be quickly expressed using 0's and 1's. For example, the BCD numbers for 2 and 4 are 0010 and 0100, respectively. Therefore, the BCD equivalent of 24 is 0010 0100.

Binary Digit: The binary digits or bits 0 and 1.

Bit: An abbreviation for binary digit.

Bug: A term for an error, defect or problem. Software bugs are errors in programs or instruction manuals. Hardware bugs are malfunctions in equipment.

Bus: A group of electrical wires or conductors that interconnect the various sections of a computer. Different computers that use the same bus can often make use of the same peripherals.

Byte: A series of eight binary bits that can indicate a number or character.

Card: A paper or plastic card containing information or program instructions. Information is encoded on paper cards by means of punched holes. Plastic cards store information as small magnetized areas in a thin film of iron oxide like that applied to magnetic recording tape.

Card Reader: A computer input mechanism capable of reading the information stored in a paper or plastic card, and feeding it into a computer.

Cassette: A cartridge containing two self-contained reels on which is wound a length of magnetic recording tape. Cassettes used to record audio information can also record and store computer data.

Central Processing Unit (CPU): The electronic nerve center of a computer. The CPU contains the arithmetic logic unit as well as the control sections that retrieve program instructions from the memory, decode them, and then execute the instructions.

Character: Usually used in reference to a character of the alphabet but sometimes used to mean any symbol, punctuation mark, letter or number that can be entered into a keyboard or displayed on a video screen.

Chip: A tiny wafer of silicon measuring a few tenths of an inch square on whose surface is etched and imprinted the hundreds or thousands of microscopic electronic components that comprise an integrated circuit (IC). The actual chip is enclosed or encapsulated within a plastic or ceramic package for protection.

Circuit: An interconnected assortment of electronic components or integrated circuit chips that together perform a recognizable operation.

Clock: An electronic circuit, often precise in nature, that emits a regulated sequence of electrical pulses synchronizing the operation of the many circuits in a digital computer.

Code: Any of numerous methods that are used to represent characters of the alphabet, digits, numbers, punctuation marks, and other symbols with binary numbers.

Compiler: A program contained within the memory of a

computer that converts a high-level computer language such as BASIC into the binary machine language that a computer understands.

Computer: An electronic device that processes information. Analog computers process approximate information; digital computers process exact information.

Control Section: The network of electronic circuits that retrieves, decodes, and carries out programmed instructions in a computer. The control section forms part of the central processing unit (CPU).

Conversational Programming: A method of programming a computer using ordinary English words and phrases. BASIC and other higher-level languages can be used to develop conversational programs.

Counter: An electronic circuit that counts incoming signals and supplies a running total in binary. Alternatively, a programmed operation that causes a computer to count for either a specified or indefinite time.

CPU: See Central Processing Unit.

Crash: A computer reaction to one or more illegal or improper program instructions. It reacts by "locking out" the keyboard and ignoring incoming commands. When a crash takes place, the computer must be reset by activating a special switch or turning the machine off and then on again. The latter operation, however, may cause the loss of whatever information is stored in the computer's memory.

CRT: An acronym for *Cathode Ray Tube*, which is the video display tube used in television sets, radar displays, and video computer terminals.

Data: Usually refers to numerical information, but may mean any kind of information fed into and read out of a computer. DATA is a BASIC computer language statement that precedes one or more pieces of numerical information in a program.

Debugging: Errors in software or hardware are called bugs. Finding and correcting bugs is the sometimes lengthy and often tedious procedure known as debugging.

Decision: An internal computer operation or programmed procedure that compares two pieces of information or verifies the status of a single piece of information, and then takes a specified action.

Decode: The process of interpreting instructions stored in a computer's memory by the central processing unit.

Digit: A single character number.

Digital Computer: An electronic system that represents numbers, symbols, and characters with two-state binary numbers and processes such information under the direction of a list of instructions stored in a memory.

Disk Memory: See Magnetic Disk Memory.

Documentation: Operating instructions, applications information, service information, programs, and other forms of software supplied with a computer or available separately.

Erase: To remove or clear information stored in a computer's memory.

Execute: To perform a specified operation listed in a program, or to run the entire program.

Flip-Flop: A simple logic circuit used in digital computers. A flip-flop can indicate binary 0 or binary 1 and can remember either a 0 or 1 as long as power is applied to the circuit.

Floppy Disk: See Magnetic Disk Memory.

Gate: The simplest electronic circuit used in a digital computer. Gates make simple decisions. Networks of gates perform more complex operations such as adding binary numbers, converting decimal numbers into binary form, decoding program instructions stored in a computer's memory, and many others.

Glitch: An unplanned and undesirable electrical pulse inside a digital computer. A glitch may occur because of improper design, or it may find its way into the computer via power lines or even through the airwaves.

Hard Copy: Computer programs, information, results, and other data printed on paper by a printer connected to a computer.

Hardware: Keyboards, video monitors, memories, circuit boards, and all other electronic circuits and equipment that form a computer.

Hexadecimal: A number system based on 16 digits that is used as a simplified way of expressing binary numbers and machine language program instructions by some hobby and single-board microcomputers.

IC: See Integrated Circuit.

Illegal Operation: An improper program instruction ordering a computer to perform an impossible operation.

Increment: To increase the value of a number, usually by one.

Integrated Circuit (IC): A microminiature electronic circuit that is imprinted and etched on the surface of a silicon chip.

Interpreter: A program stored in a computer that translates and executes a program written in a higher-level computer language one step at a time.

Interrupt: A temporary, often brief, interruption in the execution of a program so that a digital computer can handle or service an external event such as the printing of a character or the sampling of a keyboard command.

K: A common way of describing the memory capacity of a computer. K is derived from kilo and means approximately 1000 information units. An exact definition of K is 2^{10} or 1024. Therefore, an 8K computer memory can store 8192 pieces of information.

Keyboard: An array of switches that permits program instructions and numerical information to be entered into a computer manually.

Language: An organized system of words, phrases, symbols, characters, and numbers that permits a human operator to communicate with a computer and instruct it in what it is to do.

Line: A line of information in a computer program.

Line Printer: A computer printer that produces a complete line of print in one high-speed operation.

Logic Circuit: Any electronic circuit, ranging from the simplest gate to a complex microprocessor, that processes two-state binary information.

Loop: A sequence of one or more computer instructions in a program that are executed repeatedly. A loop may operate an indefinite number of times, or it may be terminated when one or more specified conditions have been met.

Machine: A microcomputer.

Machine Language: The internal binary language into which more advanced programming languages must be converted before a computer can process a computer program.

Magnetic Core: An early solid-state computer memory element consisting of a tiny donut of magnetic material that can store a single bit of data.

Magnetic Disk Memory: A computer memory that records binary information on a circular disk made of metal or plastic. Information is read from and written on the magnetic surface of the disk with a recording head similar to those used in tape recorders.

Magnetic Tape Memory: A computer memory that records binary information on magnetic recording tape.

Memory: The circuits, components or mechanical portions of a digital computer that store information.

Micro: A microcomputer.

Microcomputer: A digital computer that incorporates a microprocessor for a central processing unit. Nearly all personal computers are microcomputers.

Microprocessor: A small integrated circuit that contains the complete central processing unit for a small digital computer. A microcomputer is made by connecting a memory integrated circuit to a microprocessor.

Microsecond: A unit of time that is 1/1,000,000th of a second.

Millisecond: A unit of time that is 1/1000th of a second.

Mnemonic: An abbreviated or shorthand version of a word; a memory aid. Mnemonics are commonly used to express various machine language program instructions. For example, CLR, meaning CLEAR.

Modem: An acronym for modulate-demodulate. A circuit that permits computers to communicate with one another, often over telephone lines.

Nanosecond: A unit of time that is 1/1,000,000,000th of a second.

Nibble: A common reference to a binary number or word composed of four bits; half a byte.

Output Section: A part of a computer that makes information processed by the machine accessible to the operator or an electronic device. Typical output devices are printers and video display units.

Paper Tape: A narrow strip of coated paper into which holes are punched to represent binary information. Programs and other information can be entered into the computer's main memory by means of a paper tape and associated equipment.

Paper Tape Reader: The electromechanical apparatus that reads the information stored as perforations in a paper tape and feeds it into a computer.

Peripheral: An input or output circuit or mechanism that is designed to be connected to a computer.

Power Supply: The electronic circuits that convert the power from the household line into a form suitable for use by a computer.

Printer: A peripheral that prints programs, results of programs, and other information on either individual sheets or continuous strips of paper. Impact printers print by striking an embossed mechanism or array of pins against a carbon ribbon adjacent to the paper. Nonimpact printers print by applying heat or electricity to specially prepared papers.

Processor: A digital computer.

Program: The list of instructions that a human operator prepares to instruct a computer what to do and how to do it. See Software.

Programmable Calculator: A calculator that can be programmed much like a computer. Advanced programmable calculators can accept hundreds of program instructions, make decisions, accept programs, and other information from small, magnetic program cards and solve highly complex mathematical problems.

RAM: An acronym for random-access memory. Since read-only memories (ROMs) are random-access devices, RAM is usually employed to describe read-write memories.

Random-Access Memory: A computer memory that stores information in addresses or locations that can be accessed in the same time interval.

Read: The process of transferring information from a circuit, memory chip, punched tape, magnetic tape or floppy disk into a computer.

Read-Only Memory: A computer memory, often a solid-state integrated circuit, that stores permanent information which cannot be changed.

Read-Write Memory: A computer memory such as magnetic tape, a floppy disk or an integrated circuit whose contents can be erased and changed. Since semiconductor read-write memories are random-access devices, they are often called RAMs.

Register: A read-write memory that can temporarily store only one binary number, often an 8-bit byte.

Reset: To restore a computer to an operating state after some internal operation or illegal procedure in a program has caused the machine to crash as indicated by an unresponsive or "locked-out" keyboard.

RF Modulator: An electronic circuit that permits a computer to be connected directly to an ordinary television set to provide a convenient video display. RF modulator design is governed by restrictions imposed by the Federal Communications Commission.

ROM: See Read-Only Memory.

Run: To begin the execution of a computer program.

S-100: The name applied to the first and still one of the most popular hobby computer buses. The S-100 bus designates a row of 100 electrical contacts or conductors usually arranged as a row of 50 pairs of copper conductors along both sides of one edge of a circuit board.

Software: Documentation such as programs, lists of information, operating instructions, and other paperwork associated with the operation of a computer.

Solid State: A reference to electronic components or complete circuits made from silicon, germanium or other solid substances.

Statement: A line in a computer program such as PRINT A.

Store: To remember a piece of information.

Subroutine: One or more sequential instructions in a computer program that are ordinarily used more than once by the program. Subroutines may be as brief as several lines or they may be considerably longer than the main program that refers to them.

Teletypewriter: A computer input and output device that accepts information keyed into a typewriter-like keyboard and prints output information from the computer on a continuous roll of paper.

Terminal: An input or output peripheral connected to a computer. It usually refers to input devices with keyboards and output devices with a printer or video display unit.

Variable: In BASIC, a letter of the alphabet assigned to a memory location that can contain any designated number.

Word: A common reference to a sequence of binary bits, often an 8-bit byte, that represents a number, symbol, letter of the alphabet or program instruction. Personal computer words are usually 8 bits in length. Newer computers will use 16-bit words or 2 bytes.

Write: To store information in a memory chip, punched tape, magnetic tape or floppy disk.

Directory of
Manufacturers

AI Cybernetic Systems
   P.O. Box 4691
   University Park, NM 88003

Apple Computers
   20863 Stevens Creek Blvd.
   Cupertino, CA 95014

Centronics Data Computer Corp.
   1 Wall St.
   Hudson, NH 03051

Commodore Business Machines, Inc.
   901 California Ave.
   Palo Alto, CA 94304

Computalker Consultants
   P.O. Box 1951
   Santa Monica, CA 90406

Cromemco, Inc.
   2432 Charleston Rd.
   Mountain View, CA 94043

Cybercom (Solid State Music)
2102A Walsh Ave.
Santa Clara, CA 95050

Digital Equipment Corp.
146 Main St.
Maynard, MA 01754

Heath Co.
Benton Harbor, MI 49022

Heuristics, Inc.
900 N. San Antonio Rd.
Suite C1
Los Altos, CA 94022

Hewlett-Packard
1501 Page Mill Rd.
Palo Alto, CA 94304

Lear Siegler, Inc.
714 N. Brookhurst St.
Anaheim, CA 92803

MITS, Inc.
2450 Alamo S.E.
Albuquerque, NM 87106

MOS Technology
950 Rittenhouse Rd.
Norristown, PA 19401

Processor Technology Corp.
6200 Hollis St.
Emeryville, CA 94608

Radio Shack
1400 One Tandy Center
Fort Worth, TX 76102

RCA Solid State Division
Route 202
Somerville, NJ 08876

Soroc Technology
3074 E. Miraloma Ave.
Santa Clara, CA 95050

Southwest Technical Products Corp. (SWTPC)
219 W. Rhapsody
San Antonio, TX 78216

Teletype Corp.
5555 Touhy Avenue
Skokie, IL 60076

Texas Instruments, Inc.
Dallas, TX 75222

VideoBrain Computer Co.
150 South Wolfe Rd.
Sunnyvale, CA 94086

Index